CHICKEN SOUP FOR THE
NEW MOM'S SOUL

CHICKEN SOUP FOR THE NEW MOM'S SOUL

Touching Stories About the Miracles of Motherhood

Jack Canfield
Mark Victor Hansen
Patty Aubery

Health Communications, Inc.
Deerfield Beach, Florida

www.hcibooks.com
www.chickensoup.com

We would like to acknowledge the following publishers and individuals for permission to reprint the following material. (Note: The stories that were in the public domain, or that were written by Jack Canfield, Mark Victor Hansen, and Patty Aubery, are not included in this listing.)

The Footprint. Reprinted by permission of Paula F. Blevins. ©2006 Paula F. Blevins.

A Little Pregnant? Reprinted by permission of Stephanie Wolff Mirmina. ©2006 Stephanie Wolff Mirmina.

I'm Not Telling. Reprinted by permission of Carol Sjostrom Miller. ©2003 Carol Sjostrom Miller.

Expectant-ness. Reprinted by permission of Barbara Warner. ©2003 Barbara Warner.

. *(Continued on page 272)*

Library of Congress Cataloging-in-Publication Data

Chicken soup for the new mom's soul : stories to inspire and warm the heart of new mothers / [compiled] Patty Aubery, Jack Canfield, Mark Victor Hansen.
   p. cm.
   ISBN-13: 978-0-7573-0583-2 (trade paper)
   ISBN-10: 0-7573-0583-0 (trade paper)
   1. Motherhood—Anecdotes. 2. Mothers—Anecdotes. 3. Mother and infant—Anecdotes. 4. Mother and child—Anecdotes. I. Aubery, Patty.
II. Canfield, Jack, 1944– III. Hansen, Mark Victor.
   HQ759.C526 2007
   306.874'3—dc22

2006103119

Publisher: Health Communications, Inc.
         3201 S.W. 15th Street
         Deerfield Beach, FL 33442-8190

Cover design by Andrea Perrine Brower
Inside formatting by Anthony Clausi

*Life is a flame that is always burning itself out,
but it catches fire again every time a child is born.*

George Bernard Shaw

Contents

3. A SHOULDER TO LEAN ON

4. A MOTHER'S LOVE

5. DADDY DEAR

6. LESSONS FROM BABY

7. MOTHERHOOD 1A

8. JOYS OF MOTHERHOOD

Acknowledgments

We wish to express our heartfelt gratitude to the following people who helped make this book possible:

Our families, who have been chicken soup for our souls!

Jack's family, Inga, Travis, Riley, Christopher, Oran, and Kyle, for all their love and support.

Mark's family, Patty, Elisabeth, and Melanie, for once again sharing and lovingly supporting us in creating yet another book.

Patty's family, Jeff, J.T., and Chandler, for their love and support.

Our publisher, Peter Vegso, for his vision and commitment to bringing Chicken Soup for the Soul to the world.

Russ Kalmaski, for being there on every step of the journey, with love, laughter, and endless creativity.

D'ette Corona and Barbara LoMonaco, for nourishing us with truly wonderful stories and cartoons, and for being there to answer any questions along the way.

Patty Hansen, for her thorough and competent handling of the legal and licensing aspects of the Chicken Soup for the Soul books. You are magnificent at the challenge!

Lynn Benson, one of the coauthors of *Chicken Soup for the Soul: Life Lessons for Busy Moms*, for her useful and time-saving "Supportive Tips and Organizing Tips" through-out the book.

Veronica Romero, Teresa Esparza, Robin Yerian, Jesse Ianniello, Lauren Edelstein, Laurie Hartman, Patti Clement, Maegan Romanello, Noelle Champagne, Jody Emme, Debbie Lefever, Michelle Adams, Dee Dee Romanello, Shanna Vieyra, and Gina Romanello, who sup-port Jack's and Mark's businesses with skill and love.

Michele Matrisciani, Carol Rosenberg, Andrea Gold, Allison Janse, Katheline St. Fort, and Nancy Burke, our editors at Health Communications, Inc., for their devotion to excellence.

Terry Burke, Lori Golden, Kelly Maragni, Sean Geary, Patricia McConnell, Kim Weiss, Paola Fernandez-Rana— the sales, marketing and public relations departments at Health Communications, Inc.—for doing such an incred-ible job supporting our books.

Tom Sand, Claude Choquette, and Luc Jutras, who man-age year after year to get our books translated into thirty-six languages around the world.

The art department at Health Communications, Inc., for their talent, creativity, and unrelenting patience in pro-ducing book covers and inside designs that capture the essence of Chicken Soup: Larissa Hise Henoch, Lawna Patterson Oldfield, Andrea Perrine Brower, Anthony Clausi, and Dawn Von Strolley Grove.

Ken and Dahlynn McKowen for editing the final manuscript with such enthusiasm. Your willingness to help and your friendship mean the world to all of us.

All the Chicken Soup for the Soul coauthors who make it such a joy to be part of this Chicken Soup family.

Our glorious panel of readers who helped us make the final selections and made invaluable suggestions on how to improve the book: Catherine Barczyk, Michelle Blank, Denise Carr, Pat Cavallin, Rhonda Cordero, Gloria Dahl,

Jennifer Dale, Michele Edelstein, Dianna Foxcroft, Melanie Jonson, Renee King, Karen Kirby, Terry LePine, Swannee Rivers, Courtney Robart, Sallie Rodman, Jeanie Winstrom, Nicolle Woodward, and Deb Zika.

And, most of all, thanks to everyone who submitted their heartfelt stories, poems, quotes, and cartoons for possible inclusion in this book. While we were not able to use everything you sent us, we know that each word came from a magical place flourishing within your soul.

Because of the size of this project, we may have left out the names of some people who contributed along the way. If so, we are sorry, but please know that we really do appreciate you very much. We are truly grateful and love you all!

Introduction

For most new moms, joining the ranks of motherhood is, without a doubt, a life-changing experience.

Whether she brings her child into this world naturally or adopts her precious bundle of joy, every new mom experiences hope, hope that her child will grow to be the best person possible, to be thoughtful and kind, fun-loving and happy.

But becoming a new mom can be scary, too, as uncertainties can often bubble through at every level. *Is my baby crying too much, pooping too little, or not eating enough?* Suffice it to say, most new moms survive these fleeting moments of questioning their abilities when they witness their child thriving and growing faster than ever imagined!

Without a doubt, becoming a new mom is the most challenging and worthwhile endeavor a woman will ever face. Referring back to Shaw's quote, it is up to a new mom to fan the sparks of life and to love and nurture her child into that amazing adult-to-be.

So go ahead—light that match of new motherhood and revel in its warmth.

Share with Us

We would love to hear your reactions to the stories in this book. Please let us know what your favorite stories were and how they affected you.

We also invite you to send us stories you would like to see published in future editions of Chicken Soup for the Soul. Please send submissions to: www.chickensoup.com.

Chicken Soup for the Soul
P.O. Box 30880
Santa Barbara, CA 93130
fax: 805-563-2945

We hope you enjoy reading this book as much as we enjoyed compiling, editing, and writing it.

1

WE ARE?
YOU'RE SURE?

*Making the decision to have a child is
momentous. It is to decide forever to have
your heart go walking around outside your
body.*

Elizabeth Stone

The Footprint

"Oh," I moaned as I readjusted the pillows to accommodate my ever-growing belly. *Hadn't I just done that very thing ten minutes ago?* I sighed and rubbed my enlarged tummy. *Oh, how I missed sleeping on my stomach.*

The girl in the apartment above me was active and noisy again. It was difficult to sleep through the night during this last trimester, but with her and her visitors talking and listening to music above my head each night, it was nearly impossible.

I pulled my slumping body back up against the headboard.

My husband was at work. His hours were horrendous. I knew he'd much rather be here, but that was beyond his control. So that left me solo again. Being awake and alone this late at night, and at the end of my pregnancy, was a bad combination. Worries always seem the greatest in the dark.

What about this child inside me? Is it boy or a girl? I was pretty sure it was a girl, even though we had chosen not to officially find out from the ultrasound. Will our baby be healthy? Will we be the parents she or he needs? And what of the birth process? There was no guarantee that I could have this baby without a Cesarean. The unknown is always scary and intimidating.

With little prior knowledge of babies other than babysitting many years ago, I forced myself to read every pregnancy and parenting book and magazine for guidance through this crazy, exciting, and scary ride to becoming a mother. Everything was progressing just as all of those books said it should.

Oh, sure, there were unusual things—nosebleeds first thing every morning and crackers on the bedside table to nibble on before getting up each day so that I could rise without nausea or dizziness. And the cravings? All I ever wanted were vanilla milkshakes, and I needed them frequently. *Oh, I could sure use one of those now.*

I rolled my head toward the nightstand to see the time. The bedside clock read 2:00 AM.

If this baby stuck to pattern, it was time for the kicking show. Every four hours the child would have a grand time playing, usually at the expense of my ribs or pelvis.

I rubbed my belly again. I found myself doing that a lot lately. "Well, little one, how are you doin' in there?"

In response, I felt a kick to my right rib. "Oh, hello." The show had begun and right on time too.

Several punches to my lower abdomen followed. "Goodness, honey. You sure are getting strong."

The baby continued the gymnastics routine for several minutes. I'd push the little body back to center whenever it flopped to one side or the other.

"Oh, little one," I sighed. "I hope everything will be okay."

Suddenly all movement stopped. A tiny hard spot had formed into a funny contortion just below my left rib cage. I placed my right hand gently onto the unusual lump.

The outline was unmistakable. It was a tiny, perfect foot. I could feel the entire thing from the heel to all five toes. A new peace washed over me. Although the child could not speak, I knew in that instant that my baby was going to be okay. For with that smallest of gestures, she had placed the first of many footprints upon my soul.

Paula F. Blevins

"I wonder what causes that?"

A Little Pregnant?

I can't hear the expression: "That's like being a little pregnant" anymore without wondering. Describing something that can't be halfway—that either is or isn't—should be easy, black or white. But, there are gray areas. I spent a week inside one of them last winter.

After months of trying to conceive, finally seeing something other than that forlorn single pink line on our home pregnancy test was breathtaking. It was the secret password, the big show, the pregnancy Olympics! My husband Steve and I kissed, danced around the bathroom, and stopped to look again. But as we squinted down, it slowly dawned on us that it was not, actually, two lines but a line and a half. *A half?* We stared.

"Maybe it needs more time," Steve offered up. "Maybe we should shake it."

"It's not a Polaroid," I countered. But we re-read the directions. We waited for three more minutes, then five. Then eyeballed it off and on for an hour. Nothing. Just a line and a half.

This was uncharted territory. This was not mentioned in the fertility books that I had been reading obsessively. We waited a few days and tested again—with the same result.

"I'm sure it's just a bad batch of tests," I said this time.

"Maybe you should see the doctor," Steve said. I was already on the phone.

Two days later, as I listened on the phone to the nurse sharing my test results, I heard some other things not covered in my books: "Something wrong with the levels . . ." "Doesn't look the way it should . . ." "Too low to know for sure."

The only thing I could get out in reply was, "But, what about the second line?"

She continued, "Well, technically we're not detecting a high enough hormone level to tell if you're pregnant for sure, but there is an elevated amount, which means that you may be. We'll know more in a week when you come back to be retested."

A week? Am I or am I not? After hanging up, I felt the weight of derailed expectations swelling up inside: *But what about my breasts having gone up a cup size? I'm sleeping sixteen hours a day. I go to the bathroom four times a night. What else could it be?* And I felt different. I was just like those moms I had made fun of for saying that they knew right away. But now that it was me, I could tell something was up. And I was supposed to sit back and wait a week for my body to decide if it meant it?

While I waited for my body to decide, my mind and heart raced back over the past year. My husband and I knew we wanted children, and we knew we weren't in our twenties anymore. We started our baby quest innocently enough that summer by deciding to have a baby. Simple! We stopped using birth control and announced our intentions. This initial confidence that we'd become pregnant on demand was loosely based on my seventh grade sex-ed class, when we were warned that using fewer than three forms of contraceptives would cause us to become pregnant immediately upon having sex (or possibly the next time we thought about having sex). This proved to be the first of several misunderstandings I unquestioningly carried over from my youth.

Another was that my egg was simply hanging around midmonth waiting to be fertilized. When in reality it was like any modern woman who had things to do and a schedule to keep. If anyone wanted to see her, she'd be in her office on the third Tuesday of the month through Thursday midmorning, but really the best time for her was 10:17 AM on Wednesday unless something better came up. And if you did get in to see her, there were no guarantees. This lack of availability came as a surprise—a surprise about which no one had sat me down earlier and said, "You know, your chances of conceiving each month after the age of thirty-five are only 30 percent. Maybe you want to get going with this."

Already thirty-five, I knew every minute counted. Flash forward a few months to our new bedroom decor: basal thermometers strewn about, charts, graphs, and fertility books—dog-eared and piled high. The joy of unprotected sex had given way to phone calls saying, "Meet me at home by two o'clock today or my egg is out of here." My husband dubbed this closely monitored period of our lives as the CNN-worthy "Egg Watch 2005." Still nothing. *Were we doing it wrong?*

I started to channel conversations from wannabe grandmothers to their childless daughters everywhere: you know your eggs aren't getting any younger! It became a rallying cry echoed by subway strangers and medical personnel alike when they learned of my "advanced maternal age." While this waiting game could have been spun as an amusing diversion in our twenties (Sex! A lot of sex! Without condoms!), it now had turned into a period of self-recrimination: *What if we waited too long? What if I had waited too long? What if I can't have kids after years of trying not to have kids? What if I stood too close to that microwave back in 1995?* It belatedly began to dawn on me that I might not be in control of this biological process.

As if to confirm my self-doubt, here I was a "little" pregnant. It threw cold water on my carefully researched plans. I hadn't counted on starting out like this. There was nothing to do. *What was going on in there anyway? Had a little life taken root inside or not?* It was a mystery. In my week of hormone limbo, I stopped reading about other women's experiences and began listening to my own body. I talked to it. I whispered my hopes and spoke of our family's future plans. I looked down to find my hands rubbing my belly at unexpected moments. I replayed an almost unconscious mantra of *We're so happy to have you here. We love you and want you so much.* I tried to come to an understanding with my body that if it would support this new life inside, I would pretty much give it whatever it wanted from now on. I visualized those tiny cells growing and thriving. I caught a glimpse of the simultaneous joy and utter terror of waiting nine months without knowing or being able to control what was happening in my own body. I got ready to make room for both.

Back at the doctor's office an impossibly long week later (on my thirty-sixth birthday), I surrendered more blood and waited for the news.

"Congratulations! Let's schedule you for your first prenatal visit next month." I patted my stomach and let out the long breath I had been holding. I was ready.

Stephanie Wolff Mirmina

I'm Not Telling

When my husband and I found out that we were expecting our first child, it took us less than a day to share our news with everyone we knew. I was six weeks along, and by the time my third trimester rolled around, it seemed as if the pregnancy had lasted forever. The novelty of talking about my cravings or our nursery decorations and listening to unsolicited advice and childbirth horror stories had worn off, and I just wanted to forget about being pregnant for a while. It didn't work out that way, as everywhere I went, people looked at me in shock and said, "Haven't you had that baby yet?"

The second time around, I wanted things to be different. Sure, I was excited, but I didn't want to share it right away. I was only five weeks along and I didn't want another endless pregnancy. Plus, our four-and-half-year-old daughter, Stephanie, wasn't the most patient person in the world, so I didn't want to endure nine months of agony as she waited—and waited—for her new sibling.

Wanting Stephanie to be the first person to know about the baby, my husband and I decided not to tell anyone for three months. This amount of time sounded good since, if my history was any indication, I would start showing soon after and wouldn't be able to keep the secret much longer, and it would still give us plenty of time to prepare for the baby. Keeping our news from everyone was a necessity. We live in the small town where I grew up, and I knew that telling just one person in the strictest confidence would result in three other people approaching me at the grocery store the next day, leaning over to my daughter and announcing, "I hear you're going to be a big sister!" We didn't want to take that chance.

It wasn't easy to keep my pregnancy a secret. Whenever I had an appointment with my obstetrician (okay, I did tell one person; well, technically, he told me), I rehearsed what I would say if I knew anyone in the waiting room. And it wasn't any better at home. Although I had escaped morning sickness during my first pregnancy, this time I wasn't so lucky. I spent hours each morning—and afternoon and night—leaning over the toilet, vomiting as quietly as I could while calling out to Stephanie that I was fine. When I wasn't throwing up, I was in bed feeling as if I had gone without sleep for about a week after having been run over by a truck. There were times when I longed to call someone, anyone, and say, "I'm pregnant and I'm sick. Please take Stephanie for the day."

But I never did, because no matter how awful I felt, I loved having my little secret. Let's face it, as a mom, I didn't have many. My pregnancy and my baby hadn't yet become "public property." Nobody was telling me what to eat or warning me not to raise my arms over my head or saying, "You're going to have your hands full with two," or "Are you hoping for a boy this time?" I knew from experience that there was plenty of time for all that.

Right now, the only two people who were aware of the miracle were my husband, Jack, and I. We waited until Stephanie went to bed to share our thoughts, dreams, and excitement about our new baby—and my complaints about the pregnancy. We rubbed my belly and whispered to our baby. We schemed and planned and guarded our secret carefully, and we laughed about our "close calls," when our secret was almost discovered. All this stealth made me feel closer to my husband than I had since we had become parents.

Finally, we reached the three-month mark. After all the secrecy, I couldn't wait to share the news with Stephanie. "We have something to tell you," Jack and I said as we sat down with her. "We're going to have a new baby in our family."

Her eyes lit up. "A baby? I'm going to be a big sister?" She threw her arms around both of us. "I always wanted a baby!" she said. Then after we talked for a few minutes, she asked us to go into the kitchen because she had some things to do.

As Jack and I left the room, we heard Stephanie pushing the speed-dial button. "Granny, guess what!" she said. "We're going to have a new baby in our family! Isn't that exciting! I can't talk long because I have to call everyone I know and tell them!"

"Looks like our secret's out," Jack and I laughed as we listened to our daughter spread her happy news.

Carol Sjostrom Miller

Expectant-ness

What I remember most about the months before my daughter's arrival was the "expectant-ness" with which I lived my life.

There was the good expectant-ness, associated with the knowledge that we were about to adopt a beautiful baby girl who would forever alter the lives of my husband, my two sons, and myself. This was the one I cherished. Then, there was the not-so-good expectant-ness, associated with the knowledge that my mother, diagnosed with terminal cancer and clinging to her final few months on this earth, would probably not live to meet her new grand-daughter—a granddaughter for whom she had hoped and dreamed for years. This was the one I dreaded.

Unbelievably, it was the mingling of these two kinds of expectant-ness that helped me understand the true meaning of "expecting." I had received the call from my oldest sister, Linda, earlier that week, telling me that our mother was in the hospital again. "It didn't look good," she whispered. "Maybe you should come now, over the Thanksgiving holiday, to see her."

I was torn. I had already flown home to Indiana from Texas several times that year to see her, and my sons—

ages five and seven—were looking forward to a chance to stay home this holiday. My husband, Brian, was also weary of traveling, but he understood the predicament in which I found myself. "Go home," he said that night. "The boys and I will be just fine here. You need to be with your mom."

When I arrived at the hospital the next day, I could see that my sister had not exaggerated. Mom smiled at me weakly from her bed. "It must be bad if you returned from the sunny South," she murmured. I shrugged and joked about avoiding cooking a Thanksgiving turkey. We both settled into a comfortable silence, interrupted periodically by the beeping and clicking of the IV machine in the corner.

Finally, Mom spoke. "Tell me all about the little girl." Her eyes, overcast and dull, brightened momentarily. So did mine as I filled her in on the four-month-old baby who, sight unseen, had seized our hearts. We talked for what seemed like hours, Mom sharing her memories of the four little girls she had brought into the world. She talked about how fun it was to dress all of us and brush our hair, to share feminine wisdom and secrets. And then we were quiet again, the room swollen with the expectant-ness of a new mother and an old one, about to retire her position forever.

The doctor released our mother to my sister's home the next day, knowing there was little more he could do for her there. She had been patched up with another blood transfusion, enough to get her through the turkey and cranberry sauce, and maybe a few days besides, before her blood would again begin to fail her. We all made it through the holiday with false cheeriness, and then returned to the business of sitting around and waiting—the business of expectant-ness. A day or two later, my mother interrupted the terrible silences of the house.

"Have you bought much for the baby yet?" she asked.

I shook my head. I was an adoptive mother, having been through the state system with our sons. Our daughter would also be coming through the foster care system, and even though our experience before had been very positive, we knew better than to count on adoption paperwork always going according to plan. The less I purchased for the baby, the more secure I felt in her arrival. Call it one of those protective quirks that adoptive parents learn early on.

Mom smiled weakly, and Linda sat up straighter in her chair. "Hey! There's a baby-clothing outlet that just opened nearby! Let's go shopping!"

I hesitated. Should I explain my superstitions about shopping too early for the baby? Did I need to tell them how I was trying to protect myself, not wanting to have to bundle little pink dresses and blankets into boxes, bound for the attic, never to be used?

"That sounds like fun," Mom said quietly. I watched her eyes brighten. "Little pink dresses and booties and receiving blankets." It didn't take us long to load up her wheelchair and hit the road. We laughed and talked all the way there, remembering the shopping trips we had taken before, the bargains we had found, the lunches over which we had lingered, the chocolate sodas with which we'd end our days. This was to be our final shopping trip, a mother and her daughters, filled with expectant-ness, for the day and the promise of a new shopping companion, not yet arrived.

Mom swung into action immediately, her hands bruised from the myriad IV needles, reaching for pastel dresses with satin ribbons and flowers at the hems. She "oohed" and "aahed" over fluffy, pink blankets and hooded bath towels and caressed the brims of frilly hats, imagining, I suppose, the soft smell of the baby's head that would soon fill them. She directed my sister and me all over the store from her wheelchair perch, pointing to tiny washcloths and patterned sleepers. The life in her eyes buoyed me and carried me from my feeling of despair. I was an expectant mother, she bragged to every salesclerk in the store. We were going to have a baby girl in the family, and she would need to be dressed to the nines.

We went home that night and pulled our soft, pink treasures from a sea of bags that covered the living room floor. I watched my mother's watery eyes travel over each tiny outfit, and then light on me with a smile. The torch had been passed.

My daughter, Ellie, arrived two months later, three weeks after my mother finally lost her fight with cancer. I wrapped my baby lovingly in each of those beautiful dresses and remembered that last shopping trip with my mother that showed me the real meaning of expectantness. On that day, I learned that expecting is more than waiting for something to happen. On that day, it was about living in the moments between.

Barbara Warner

Beautiful Mess

Pregnancy is one of the most extreme times in a woman's life: extreme emotions, extreme moods, extreme appetite. I remember being so tired, but also incredibly ambitious. I was nervous about the baby's health, doctor's visits, needles, and weight gain, and yet I understood real hope for the first time in my life. And in the midst of pregnancy, when I became heavier than ever before, I somehow felt more beautiful than any previous time in my life. This body, which society says must be thin to be fashionable and is for display purposes only, now had real purpose.

There are so many joys along the road to becoming a new mother—the least of which is the many people who love to tell you every little negative thing that happened to them during pregnancy, childbirth, and those blessed first months with a new baby. You announce your due date and everyone says, "Congratulations," right before they jump into their own story about their fifty-hour unmedicated labor, followed by thirteen weeks of straight colic, teenage angst, and how they cannot get their grown children to leave home.

I *love* the special people in my life who tell me, "You're

as big as a house" or "Enjoy sleep while you can." They show the emotional sympathy of a hungry pit bull.

But I want you to know that no matter the pains or discomforts or fears, there will be no time in your life as sweet. Nothing will bring such a beautiful smile or fonder memories than when you think back to preparing for your baby. If the road to becoming a mom were not as difficult as it is joy-filled, then we would take it for granted. It is the aches and pains and little quirky weird things that happen along the way that make our stories unique, that tie us to our children with such fierceness. We know what it cost to get them here. The rough edges of pregnancy are smoothed out by intense love and joy. For example: there is nothing like the first kicks of your baby in the womb. Of course, if you've made it to the seventh month or beyond, you will occasionally wish junior wasn't so aggressive. My first child wedged his feet into my ribs so hard I was sure he was trying to break out early. Because of this, I often said that I would be so much happier with a baby in my arms rather than karate-chopping my insides. The things that were so hard to endure in the long minutes of every day become the things you miss as time moves on. Two months after my son was born, I became a liar. I missed his little kicks terribly. I missed his flip-flopping in the night. I had to have another one so I could feel it again.

No matter how many absolutely adorable pictures you get at Sears or Penney's, they will never bring the feeling those first ultrasound pictures bring. There is such an intense rush in knowing that there really is a baby growing inside you, and it's your son or daughter! You can actually see them suck their thumbs or tickle their own toes. For me it was proof; it seemed to take the abstract and bring it all home. This confirms your motherhood: you must now wear jeans that rise above the belly button (just kidding).

Here's the best part: all the leg shaving, makeup wearing, bikini waxing, eyebrow plucking, high-heel walking, and hair fixing you've ever done or had to learn how to do; all the rude stares, catcalls, impolite gestures, and unequal treatment; anything and everything that makes being a woman hard, inconvenient, and tiresome—even pregnancy and labor—comes crashing down when you, at your weakest, become the strongest you've ever been and push your child into this world, and you finally embrace the beautiful, messy joy that is your newborn.

As I stared at my son's quivering lips while he cried in the first minutes after he was born, I was so proud. I was proud to be a woman, and no amount of pain or fear or stereotype placed upon me by society would ever change that again. I alone was equipped to care for and give birth to this boy. My body nurtured him for nine months and would keep fat on his thighs for a year more through breast-feeding.

It is an empowering feeling. We are told there are so many things we can't do, and then we realize we are capable of the seemingly impossible. We triumph in the face of unspeakable difficulties!

And what they say is true! We forget the hardest parts of pregnancy, at least enough to go through it again. But God made pregnancy hard for a reason—nobody but a tired, pregnant woman could actually look forward to labor.

Heather Best

Unplanned Blessings

It was the tiniest thing I ever decided to put my whole life into.

Terri Guillemets

I looked up from the waiting room chair and nodded to the nurse. Gathering up my purse I followed her into the small clinic exam room, my stomach in knots.

"The test came back positive. You're pregnant." She motioned me to a chair and I sat down heavily. For many women, those few words would be cause for celebration, kicking off a nine-month period of expectant planning and joyful discovery. But I was twenty years old and unmarried. To say I hadn't planned for this was an understatement.

"A counselor will be in shortly to discuss the options with you." The nurse was matter-of-fact as she hung my chart on the door and walked out. I looked around the sparsely furnished room, hoping I wouldn't have to throw up before we were done talking. Lately I couldn't keep anything down. Now I knew why.

A few minutes later a kind-looking woman entered the

room and sat down opposite me. She introduced herself and began asking questions, questions I didn't want to answer.

"Catherine, is the baby's father supportive?" I stared blankly at her. He hadn't exactly been planning for this either.

She calmly outlined the options as my mind raced. None of them sounded good. I avoided her eyes when it was time to go, feeling stupid and immature.

In the parking lot I got in my car and just sat, staring out the window. A few blocks away was the Pacific Ocean. I could just make out the water, glinting in the setting sun. My boyfriend and I enjoyed going for walks on the beach and trying to jump the waves that came crashing in. We'd return to the car soaking wet, the warmth of sunburn fighting off the chill. Life had been fun, carefree. But not anymore. I turned the key, tears burning behind my eyes.

I never dreamed about getting married and starting a family. In school, home economics class seemed like a waste of time. There were too many things I wanted to do: travel, see the world, and establish myself in a career. Children were the last thing on my mind. Now I was faced with decisions I wasn't ready to make and there was nobody to blame but myself.

In my fourth month I told my family about the pregnancy. At my mother's suggestion I moved back home and began working as a receptionist in a doctor's office. I watched my body begin to change.

Nothing about the pregnancy seemed to go easily. My morning sickness didn't stop at the end of my first trimester; I threw up morning, noon, and night well into my sixth month. The nausea wore off just in time for painful indigestion that required prescription medication. Then I was plagued by fluid retention that became so bad in the summer heat that all I could wear on my feet were flip-flops. By the third trimester I gazed helplessly at my bloated reflection in the bathroom mirror. My body felt out of control, just like my life.

One night in the eighth month, exhausted after a long day, I peeled off my clothes and ran a bath. The baby felt heavy, on my mind as well as on my body. I poured fragrant bubble bath into the warm water and watched as the bubbles foamed up.

Carefully I lowered myself into the water and lay my head back on a small pillow. I looked at my belly, rising out of the bubbles like a barren island. As I ran my fingers over it, I felt the baby move and watched as the outline of a limb pressed against my hand. Wonder at the baby growing inside filled my heart. Consumed with worries and discomforts, I often forgot that soon a small person would be sharing my life. I wondered about our future together.

Like the pregnancy, my delivery did not go smoothly. At two weeks overdue the doctor induced labor. Twelve hours later, nothing had happened.

"We'll try again next week; the baby's just not ready." The doctor seemed unconcerned. A nurse shut off the Pitocin drip and removed the IV so I could return home. Fighting despair, I pulled the maternity pants up over my aching belly. Nothing was going right. Even my baby didn't want to be born.

It seemed almost unbelievable that a week later, following sixteen hours of labor pain unabated by an epidural, I delivered a healthy baby boy. When the nurse placed my son in my arms I looked at him in awe. Running my fingers over his dark wisps of hair, I examined the small hands and feet. Despite the hardships, my baby was born perfectly put together.

Six weeks later I called the pediatrician to make an appointment.

"We have your son scheduled for a checkup next Tuesday at 9:00 AM" I wrote down the date. My son. The words were new to my lips, foreign and wonderful at the same time. I had a son to love, care for, and be delighted by. For the rest of my life.

The joy of motherhood took me completely by surprise. The difficult pregnancy and early fears began to fade away as I experienced the incredible feeling of falling in love with my own child. I didn't know how wonderful it would feel to snuggle the warm weight of an infant or see his small head turn at the sound of my voice. No one told me I could gaze for hours at my baby's face or jump out of a perfectly warm bed to stand by his crib and listen to him breathe. Mothering, as it turned out, was a journey my heart wanted to take.

Catherine Madera

[Author's Note: *There were other blessings, too, when I married my baby's father. Five years later we added a daughter to our family. Life, in its healing way, moved on. Twelve years have now passed and my son is growing tall, his face just beginning to lose the roundness of childhood. His features are an intriguing mix of genetics: deep black-brown eyes from a Portuguese great grandfather, the expressions of his dad, and from me, fair skin with a sprinkling of freckles. When I look at him I am reminded that life is a gift. And that sometimes, unplanned events bring us great joy.*]

I Want My Mom!

Thousands of miles from home, in a tiny Alaska frontier town, a rainbow of eight dilapidated trailers stretched a quarter mile down a gravel road. Sheila and her soldier husband lived in the old red one, and I lived in the faded green. Sheila preceded me to Alaska by three months. She knew what it felt like to be the most recent military bride to arrive, so when our husbands left for work, she strolled the weathered, wooden boardwalk that connected the trailers and came to welcome me. Her Boston brogue was as difficult for me to decipher as my Midwest accent was for her. We made small talk. She told me that she had a "cedah chest full of pattuhns" back home. I asked what a "pattuhn" was. She repeated herself loudly, but my dumbfounded expression told her I didn't understand. She spelled, "P-a-t-t-e-r-n," and I laughed.

"Oh, of course, yes, I sew too," I responded. Thus began a supportive friendship. We walked a half-mile to town; she gave me the grand tour. I registered at the closet-sized general delivery post office and browsed next door in the combination grocery and general store located on the main highway. We discovered that we had more in common: same former occupation, same shoes, same likes and dislikes, and the same way of thinking. Our friendship was sealed with hilarity when we walked the footpath behind our trailers and spied two lime green nightgowns blowing in the breeze, one hanging on her clothesline and the other on mine. We laughed ourselves silly.

We were barely out of high school when we became brides and still newlyweds when our husbands were drafted. After they completed their training, we accompanied them to their duty post. We lived off base, in Delta Junction, where a herd of buffalo meandered through town, moose ambled along the tree line, and black bear were frequently sighted foraging among the forest of stunted trees across the road from us.

Two months after my arrival, Sheila drove me to the army dispensary for a required medical checkup, and she waited in the reception area. After my exam I came out beaming with an ear-to-ear grin and a printed list of nutritional requirements for expectant mothers.

"Oh my gawd! Are you pregnant, too?" Our due dates were two months apart. "Did you read that list? Fresh fruit in rural Alaska, and look at how many servings of vegetables we need. Milk? Forget it! It's unaffordable; everything has to be trucked or flown in," she frowned.

I had already discovered that budgeting on a military salary was like tying shoes with laces too short. We never seemed to make ends meet, and by payday we could not afford six cents for a postage stamp to write home.

Winter set in. Sadness and lethargy engulfed me as my hormones went haywire. I felt like I was a million miles from home. I wanted my mom. *How would I ever survive in minus fifty-degree temperatures and eighteen hours of darkness each day?*

Sheila came to my rescue. Shortly after our husbands left for work each day, we sat in each other's kitchen, and for three hours we talked, played Yahtzee, made stuffed animals out of felt squares, and filled them with toilet tissue. Then it was time to walk to the post office. We put on our furry parkas and boots and trekked to town. We deliberately pooched out our bellies, proud of our expanding girth. As we spoke, our breath crystallized and hung in midair like small clouds. We warmed up in the general store and browsed in the infant's department. We yearned for the crib blankets. I oohed and ahhed over the yellow one with kittens and she liked the one with pink lambs. We discovered matching stuffed animals. Sheila picked up the musical pink lamb and twisted the tiny key on its side. I wound up the yellow kitten and watched its head rotate from side to side. We held them to our ears and listened to the lullabies every single day; we nearly wore them out. We wished our way through the rack of unaffordable maternity outfits. If only we had enough money.

One day we squealed with delight when I discovered two crisp dollar bills tucked inside a letter from my mom. We knew that we should have bought fruits and vegetables, especially since our diets consisted mainly of ground beef, eggs, and tuna, but the desire for chocolate was mind-altering. We darted to the refrigerated case and purchased a Sara Lee chocolate cake. We were addicted, but we were also penniless.

The following day, as we browsed in Diehl's General Store, I spied a hand-lettered sign that stated that military personnel were eligible to run a credit tab in the food department. I told my husband that expectant mothers required more nutrition, and I persuaded him to open an account. The next day Sheila and I were like two children in a candy store. I made the first purchase, another chocolate cake and a quart of milk. Again Sheila and I devoured the cake in one sitting and buried the foil pan in the bottom of the outdoor trash barrel.

Our prenatal visits, which began at Fort Greely with a

weigh-in, always ended in celebration with a chocolate cake. My husband paid the tab each month, unaware that we had been fudging the bill.

Spring arrived with warmer temperatures, longer days, and fields of pink wildflowers. We traipsed along the winding paths in the woods, the tundra moist and spongy beneath our feet. We rested our folded arms on our swollen abdomens and wondered and worried aloud: "What will it be like to be a mother? I hope I can give this baby everything it needs. We don't even have enough money for a crib blanket."

As Sheila's due date neared, we decided to splurge, neglected a utility payment, and purchased the baby blankets and animated stuffed animals. We walked home rubbing the soft fabric on our cheeks, listening to the tinkling lullabies and beautiful music.

Sheila had a baby girl. A few weeks later, I gave birth to my daughter. We shared our first taste of motherhood in her kitchen as we shoveled rice cereal and formula into our baby's mouths and chocolate cake into ours.

I never knew being a mom would be so hard. I never slept. My baby was so colicky. She was so constipated. *What was I doing wrong?*

After nearly two years in Alaska, we returned home to Boston and St. Louis where we reared our families and maintained a long-distance friendship. Sheila and I often return to Alaska, if only in our memories. During the past thirty-six years we have tied the loose ends of youth into an everlasting friendship knot. If we had known then what we know now, that pregnancy and motherhood are often as beautiful as Alaska's spring wildflowers, and sometimes as confusing and confining as the narrow wilderness paths we walked so many years ago, we would do it all again. We have cradled our babies and our daughters' babies.

I have come to understand that the blanket one chooses to wrap her newborn in isn't as important as swaddling them in love. Having a supportive friend to share the joys, trials, and tribulations is undoubtedly the best gift a new mother can receive.

Linda O'Connell

Number five and number six have been delightful. I didn't feel complete at six, but I couldn't fathom having any more, either. We were busy with a major relocation and I was working on a book launch, and the thought of having to endure another uncomfortable pregnancy was more than I could handle. The more time went on, the more accustomed to the idea we became of perhaps finally moving on to the next chapter in our lives. *Were the child-bearing years over for us?* I was only thirty-three, so I wasn't so sure, but I was certainly not ready to have another. Maybe we would adopt, spare my body the stress, and still grow the family until I felt complete again.

My husband grew ever more fond of the idea of being finished. In fact, as time went on it became a touchy issue, and though I didn't feel entirely complete, he didn't like discussing it. He felt that we weren't good enough to handle more than the ones we already had. I felt like we'd grow with it if we allowed ourselves the opportunity.

Over time, I came to terms with the fact that I couldn't be the only one to think about having another—if he was done, I should let it go. After all, I believed our relationship needed to come first, and I really didn't want to go through pregnancy again anyway. If ever I felt incomplete, I would remind myself that I chose to respect my husband's concerns and preserve our relationship.

Just when I had come to terms with this and was looking toward all the things we could do as a family with our last child only a few months from being diaper free, my period failed to arrive. *I must be off schedule,* I thought. But when it didn't come after a whole week, the truth began to settle in. I was numb and didn't know what to think. After all that I had wrestled with in trying to decide, the decision had already been made, and my husband didn't even know. *How was I going to tell him?* He'd be so discouraged and overwhelmed! I took a home pregnancy test and have never seen a darker, surer indication that confirmed it was true.

We were at a hotel on a business trip together, and I was preparing to give a presentation that evening. I wondered, *how long could I keep it a secret, and under what circumstances would I have the courage to break it to him? Could I hide it for three or four months? Could I prepare him for this announcement? Might his attitude change between now and then?*

But I've never been good at keeping such a thing secret. Finally I got the courage to let him know. A grin spread over my face. I couldn't keep a straight look, and he said, "What?"

I couldn't say anything. Finally I said, "Houston, we have a situation."

He asked what I meant, and I hesitated so long that he began to look worried. He couldn't tell if I had good news or bad, or how serious it would be. I thought he'd guess it just by how I was acting, but he was completely in the dark. I said, "Remember last time when I told you we didn't need protection?"

He waited.

I continued, "It's because we were already pregnant."

I braced myself for him to close his eyes, breath a heavy sigh, and groan a deflated "Oh, no" reaction.

Instead, his eyes became wide, he leaned in, and a smile spread across his entire face. Tears of joy filled his eyes, and I cannot remember him ever beaming so proudly as he did then! The love and adoration he felt for me at that moment shone in his eyes and he embraced me tenderly, thrilled at the news.

I pulled back saying, "What?" Waving my hand back and forth I continued, "What is this all about? If you were going to feel this way, why were you so adamant against the idea in the first place?"

He explained that if God wanted to send us another

child, he was all for it. But he hadn't felt prepared to make that decision himself. To have it happen so unexpectedly was precisely how it needed to happen. As my husband and I rejoiced together, and with number seven on the way, I finally felt complete.

Kaye Robertson

A Joyous Journey

[Authors' Note: *May 18, 2006: Mark graduates from high school and is accepted to Washington University in St. Louis, College of Arts & Sciences, The January Program.*]

Drift back nineteen years ago:

As I slowly made the turn into our driveway, I saw that the garage door was open, and there stood my husband of four years. It was a cold, windy day in March 1987, and he was wearing a stocking cap. That's about all I remember. I'm sure he must have had on a coat or jacket, but all I remember is that knitted cap. I rolled to a stop, put my car in park, pulled the emergency brake, and just sat there for a moment while his eyes met mine. He looked at me with an inquisitive look and raised his eyebrows, as if to say, "Well? What did you find out?" I picked up the book from the passenger seat that the doctor had given me during my appointment. I held it up to the windshield with the title side facing him. His expression changed from curious to disbelief to shock in the two or three seconds it took me to begin crying . . . again! The name of that book was *Pregnant and Lovin' It.*

We had not planned on having a child of our own. We both had been married once before. He had two sons: Ron, Jr., age twenty, and Matt, age sixteen. I had one son, Scott, age fourteen. For one thing, we were too old, or so it seemed! We were dealing with teenage boys and trying to "semi" blend our sons into a family. (And as I've professed many times since then: "Real life is not like the Brady Bunch!")

But as it happened, it seemed like there was another "PLAN" for our lives that we weren't aware of at the time.

Some things were happening to me, or not happening as it were, so I made an appointment with my gynecologist. On March 30, 1987, the doctor uttered in his charming British accent those now infamous words, "My dear, you're pregnant!" *What??? How can this be?? How did this happen??* All those ridiculous, rhetorical questions kept repeating themselves in my head. I was still deep in thought when I sat in our driveway, gazing at Ron. I don't believe I will ever forget that image of him. It was as if the outline of the garage was a stage and he was part of the play.

It only took me twenty-four hours to arrive at the final emotions: Joy and Happiness! I was thrilled with the idea that I was going to have another baby! *Did I want another boy? I loved little boys! Or did I want a little girl, since our family was already full of boys? It didn't matter, as long as the baby was healthy.*

After my emotional roller-coaster ride, the calendar date showed April 1. I telephoned all my family and long-distance friends and began the conversation with these words, "This is NOT an April Fool's joke. I am pregnant!"

Those months of pregnancy were some of the happiest of my life. I hadn't felt so healthy and full of energy in a long time; and I ate everything in sight! Even though the technology was already available to detect the baby's sex before it was born, Ron and I decided to be old-fashioned, wait, and be surprised.

On October 20, 1987, Mark was born by a scheduled C-section. Another boy! We were thrilled! Ron was able to be in the operating room with me, and I was so very happy that he was able to share this miracle with me. But, the nurses whisked Mark away, and soon we were told that our baby had some fluid in his lungs and wasn't breathing properly. He had to be kept in a special area of the nursery, in something similar to an oxygen tank, with tubes attached in various places. It was heartbreaking, not being able to hold and cuddle him. Ron and I would walk down the hallway to see him, to touch his little fingers and toes, but weren't allowed to hold him or give him a bottle. I begged my doctor to let me stay in the hospital until Mark was well enough to come home. But insurance companies have their rules. I was forced, for lack of a better word, to leave the hospital without my newborn son.

After arriving home, all I could do was gaze at Mark's new crib and caress all his tiny clothes. I said about a million prayers, asking for a miracle, if that's what it was going to take to bring him home.

Astonishingly, he began to improve immediately, and we were told we could take him home on October 26, which was only two days after my release. Joy set in, but also fear. *What if he really wasn't ready to be released from the hospital? What if he needed the expert care that he could only receive there?* The nurses assured both Ron and me that our baby was fine and ready to go home with his adoring, devoted, and doting parents! Bringing him home was one of the happiest days of our lives. We would jokingly argue over whose turn it was to hold him and give him his bottle, even those middle-of-the-night feedings! We both loved him so intensely.

We raised him with love and compassion. We demonstrated our spiritual faith and also displayed our faith in him. We always expressed our belief that he could accomplish anything he truly wanted in his life.

Fast-forward back to graduation night:

He's made us extremely proud, and the future can only hold fabulous things for him. What a wonderful gift we received all those years ago!

Becky Povich

Twice Blessed

*Therefore, encourage one another and build
each other up, just as in fact you are doing.*
1 Thessalonians 5:11

For ten years, as we watched our friends have children, Richard and I had prayed that we'd become parents. Throughout the sorrows of a false pregnancy and lost dreams, God showed us that hope was not lost as we were accepted into an adoption program.

We spent six months taking parenting classes, filling out paperwork, and agonizing over home visits from our caseworker. When everything was completed and we were approved, months went by as we were considered for one child or another, but always passed over. Somehow, I believe God had a very special child in mind for us.

Nine months after we began classes, ironic in God's joyous ways, the call we'd waited for came.

"Her name is Michelle," our caseworker said. On that day, November 2, 1991, we learned of our imminent adoption of our nine-month-old daughter. And her birth name was Michelle, the name we'd chosen for our first child twelve years earlier before we were married.

It was time to celebrate. As promised, we called our closest friends and treated them to a special celebration dinner. While we laughed and talked at the restaurant, telling them what we knew about our soon-to-arrive and much-prayed-for daughter, I became aware that the older couple in the booth behind us laughed as we did and nodded knowingly as we voiced our excitement and nervousness.

We weren't quiet. We were full of joy at the good news. It bubbled over as we talked and planned in the restaurant.

"What if we're not good parents?" I asked.

"What if the adoption doesn't go through and we lose her after we've fallen in love?" Richard asked.

"I bet she's sweet and adorable and full of smiles," I said.

"I bet she'll be a daddy's girl," Richard said.

The louder we got, the more I noticed how quiet the older couple became. But I was too excited to worry, too scared to stop talking.

When the couple behind us left their booth, they paused at our table.

"Congratulations," the woman said, patting my shoulder.

"Thank you," I said, grateful that they weren't angry at our loudness.

She leaned closer. "We have a granddaughter who was adopted by a couple not long ago. I've never seen her. Hearing your excitement, I feel in my heart that somewhere she is loved and well taken care of by a family like you." Patting my shoulder once more, she whispered, "I'll pray for you and your baby."

At a time when we were blessed and overflowing with joy, God put us in a place where we could be a blessing and comfort for another. As our conversation encouraged her, this woman took a moment to stop and encourage my heart.

I prayed for that grandmother, that God gave her peace and comfort for the granddaughter she wondered about. And I knew that my husband and I were in her prayers that night.

Kathryn Lay

Passing the Baton

My daughter recently hosted a baby shower for a friend
from work. She decorated the living room with blue and
pink streamers and baked a cake in the shape of a baby
carriage. Everything looked beautiful. As I watched her
welcome her guests and fuss with the table, I thought
about the shower my friends had hosted when I was
expecting her—it felt like yesterday. I realized in an unset-
tling moment that I was old enough to be this baby's
grandmother, and something inside me began to ache.

Since the birth of my children I have been so intent on
the day-to-day that I've misplaced years, even decades.
The passage of time warped with their arrival, and they
grew up in a beat of my heart. I can't remember the last
diaper I changed or bottle I warmed. The preschool years
have melted into a smear of finger paints, baseball seasons
have disappeared in the time it takes to run the bases,
hours spent at the skating rink spin away in a blink of an
eye. Their first steps, their first teeth, their first day at
school, first dates and graduations, recitals, concerts,
hockey games, tap shoes, skates, skis—all the props of
their childhood rattle in my mind.

I watched the mother-to-be unwrap her gifts, the swell

of her stomach resting on her knees. She absently patted the bulge of her unborn child and my memory mimicked the same motion. Pregnancy is not easily forgotten.

As the last gift made its way around the room, the young women settled into their tea and cake. The conversation shifted, as it always does at showers such as this, to the maternity ward and tales of long nights and labor. The expectant mother's eyes grew round as she listened to increasingly vivid recollections of delivery room horrors. It was as if the baton was being passed from one mother to the next as they competed in the Olympics of childbirth.

It appears that regardless of the age of the child, its birth can generally be recalled in moment-by-moment glory, every detail, every pain. And our eagerness to share the experience seems second only to our need to relive it ourselves. It's as if mothers are members of an elite club and obligated to initiate new members by scaring them to death.

At eight-and-a-half months pregnant the guest of honor's fate was sealed. She will deliver her baby regardless of what happens during the process. She will join the club and begin an adventure that will be long on days and disappear faster than she can possibly imagine. Before she knows it she'll be old enough to be somebody's grandmother and reliving her own story.

Elva Stoelers

Organizing Tips

- Pack weeks in advance! Ideas of what to bring to the hospital include:

  ✓ Toiletries

  ✓ Cosmetics

  ✓ Bathrobe and slippers

  ✓ Multiple pairs of underwear (if hospital doesn't provide the special netting underwear) and a few pairs of warm socks

  ✓ Sanitary pads (have some on hand even though hospitals usually provide)

  ✓ Nursing bras if breast-feeding

  ✓ Comfortable clothes to wear home

  ✓ A couple of baby sleepers, as well as baby clothes, hat, and warm blanket for the trip home

  ✓ Some receiving blankets (although most hospitals provide them)

  ✓ Newborn diapers (although most hospitals provide them)

  ✓ Insurance information for the hospital; magazine and books

2

THE BIG DAY

*A new baby is like the beginning of all things—
wonder, hope, a dream of possibilities.*

Eda LeShan

The Right Stuff

I just had to have a girl as my first child, because I had created her name when I was just a girl myself.

My parents named me Dahlynn, pronounced "Da-Lin" with the accent on the second syllable. In my family, the girls are named after others in the family—male or female —never using the same name, but a combination of those names. The first part of my name comes from my grandmother DeEtta, and the second half from my uncle's middle name, Lynn. The boys in our family had an easier time, as they were given common names and not expected to keep the tradition going, even if they had daughters.

Having this family tradition handed down to me was a big cross to bear. I started creating names for my future daughter in fourth grade, working on word and name combinations from past generations. Every time I created a new name, I added it to the growing stack of names hidden in my small jewelry box.

Finally I had the perfect name—Lahre, which rhymed with "Marie." The "Lah" came from the "Dah" in my name, and the "re" from the end of my mother's name, Scharre. I was only in seventh grade when I placed that name in my box.

Fortunately, I waited until I graduated from college and married before I became pregnant at the age of twenty-eight. In all that time I never thought of a name for a boy, only for a girl.

Needless to say, I was excited about the pregnancy, even with the constant nausea and everything that came with it. We decided to go the old-fashioned route—no, not a natural delivery—we decided to not find out the sex of the baby. We wanted to be surprised, and I was so sure it was a girl that there was no reason to find out.

Once I started to really show, it became obvious that I was carrying the baby to the front. "That's a sign it's a boy," is all I heard from friends and family, even strangers. *No, it can't be a boy!* I screamed in my head, while on the outside I smiled and quietly nodded when told I was having a boy.

The nine months went by slowly and they were mostly wonderful, after I got past the nausea. Each and every day I would talk to my little girl, sharing with her my dreams for her, even placing headphones on my stomach and playing all kinds of music. But again, since I was carrying the baby to the front, people tried to tell me I was having a boy. Slowly I started to believe them, and when the time came to go to the hospital, I was torn. We picked out a name for a boy—Christopher—after General H. Norman Schwarzkopf's son. My husband had heard Schwarzkopf's son mentioned in an interview; the year was 1992 and Schwarzkopf was leading our troops in Desert Storm.

The delivery was anything but ordinary. I was two weeks overdue, and after sixteen very hard hours of back labor, with my husband and my amazing seventy-year-old grandmother DeEtta (my namesake) by my side, the doctor decided to do a C-section.

Once prepped in the operating room and with a sheet placed in front of my face so I couldn't watch, the doctors began the procedure. My grandmother was extremely curious as to what the doctors were doing, asking about this and that. My husband was watching, too, and when they pulled my stomach out and set it on top of my chest, he about fainted. The nurse had him sit back down in the chair, which was placed next to my head. I looked up and saw he was white as a ghost.

Finally, the doctor said, "Here's the baby!" The doctor placed the crying baby up over the sheet so we both could see it, and my husband said, "Oh, look at the little guy." *A boy? We have a boy?* I said to myself. But then the doctor said, "It's not a boy . . . it's a girl!" My husband had mistaken the large umbilical cord for a "manly attribute"!

Our amazing son, Shawn, would show up five years later, and again we didn't find out the sex until he was born. I didn't listen when I was told I was going to have a girl the second time; I knew I was having a boy because I grew lots of facial hair! But my daughter Lahre is my special joy, even as she is now facing her teenage years. And guess what? She keeps her stash of names for her future daughter in a little jewelry box.

Dahlynn McKowen

Better than Expected

Babies are a bit of stardust blown from the hand of God. Lucky is the woman who knows the pangs of birth for she has held a star.

Larry Barretto

"Do you know what it is?" the mailman asked, reaching out of his window, opening the door to our mailbox. Considering the fact that my middle was the size of a one-person dome tent, I assumed he was inquiring about the baby, not the letter he delivered.

"Don't know," I responded. "It'll be a surprise, I guess. But I'm pretty sure it's not a large amphibian or a small kitchen appliance."

Surprise wasn't the word for this pregnancy. Shock, maybe. Stunned, perhaps. But more than surprise.

When my husband, Dave, and I married fourteen years ago, we discussed how many children we'd like to have. "Let's just take it one at a time," was my husband's advice. So, one at a time they came: in 1993, in 1995, in 1997, in 1998, and now one due in 2001.

How this baby was conceived was an anomaly. Dave

argues that it was the mailman's baby, which may explain the undue concern by the aforementioned mailman. The kids said Dave and I must have swapped chewing gum. I calculated, using a highly sophisticated mathematical formula, that conception must have occurred sometime between brushing my teeth on a Tuesday morning in March and driving to the grocery store on a Saturday evening in April. There was really no way of knowing for sure—just one of those virgin conception things.

The first five months of my pregnancy, I stubbornly slid on my skinny jeans and bound them at the button with a ponytail holder. It was kind of like stretching the mouth of an empty water balloon over the spout on the kitchen faucet. "Puuuuullll! A little mooooore! There!" Until I grew the size of a European motorcar, I just couldn't bring myself to wear those pregnant pants with the stomach area lined with itchy, stretchy polyester.

Nor could I bear to hear total strangers—the single guy in line at the gas station, a librarian struggling with infertility—mouths agape, gasp, "Another one?"

Worse yet were the nonstrangers—former colleagues at work, old college roommates (childless by choice) spewing, "Don't you know how to stop this?"

I received one pseudopositive remark during my pregnancy from our tax consultant: "If you push this kid out by December 31, you'll get another . . . (tap, tap, tap on the calculator) . . . sixteen dollars!" *Great. With the additional income I could purchase enough disposable diapers to last the new baby, what . . . four hours?*

Snide remarks aside, our family was pretty excited about the prospect of having another baby. Especially, perhaps, a boy baby. After all, we had monopolized the XX chromosome market with our four daughters. Maybe this time we'd get a son.

Our family spent the next few months preparing for our new arrival. With four little girls, this meant devising a "holding schedule" that dictated who would get to hold the new baby for how long and under what circumstances: 1) No holding the baby while any bodily fluid slides out of your nose; 2) No carrying the baby around in a Strawberry Shortcake suitcase; and 3) No touching the baby's face while finger painting the dog.

On those long sleepless nights in the third trimester when my breath was compressed by the weight of three minivans (or one nine-pound baby), I'd pray, "Dear God, please let this baby be healthy, easy, and resilient. And if you could give it a penis, that'd be great too."

Then one December night, way too close to Christmas, labor began. Mild, at first, like an I-played-tennis-too-long-yesterday backache, then stronger. Soon contractions wrung my back like a wet dish towel. I knew that sensation all too well. The sensation of living for two people at once. A payment of pain for potential. A trade of love for life.

"I don't want to do this again," I groaned to Dave. But I knew from experience that all I could do at this point was sleep when I could, cry when I must, and when the time came, push like there was no tomorrow.

Tomorrow. *Tomorrow I'll be holding a sweet, fresh ball of baby all tidy and sweet. And it will be good, so good,* I reminded myself. But first I had to get through today.

And today meant walking miles on the hospital's cold tile floors. It was hours of work. And that sterile smell hospitals exhale: antiseptic and latex and sick. So many monitors beeping and nurses prodding and clocks with hands that never seem to move. Then . . .

"It's time," my midwife whispered. "Your baby's coming, Cristy. You can push." Pressing her face close to mine, she looked me hard in the eyes and spoke slowly, enunciating each syllable: "Your body can do this. Everything's fine."

Delirious with pain, in the throes of excruciating two-minute-long contractions, I panted, "What? Ubangi's canoe with a venomous swine?"

Dave laughed. The midwife laughed. Some nurse with really bad breath laughed. I, in turn, pushed out a baby—not laughing, I might add.

My baby felt like a lump of moist Play-Doh plopped on my flabby belly. Only warmer. It didn't cry, only squirmed against my naked skin, searching to suck and snuggle.

"You can check, Dad." The midwife encouraged Dave. Gently, like he would the wing of a resting butterfly, my husband lifted the baby's little leg and checked.

Pushing his face into my damp hair my husband whispered, "She's perfect."

Today, years later, when I recall Lydia's birth, I think about a higher purpose. When I ask each of my five daughters what she may someday choose to do with her life, one will say, "I might want to become a scientist." Another, "I want to coach basketball." My third, "I want to become an otolaryngologist." And a fourth, "A mom, definitely."

But Lydia? When I ask my little Lydia what she will contribute to this world, she just smiles her special smile and replies, "Don't know. It'll be a surprise, I guess."

Cristy Trandahl

First Night Home

Our first night home.

With you in a cradle beside our bed, your father and I discovered that our box springs were much louder than we ever expected. Between this squeaking, your hunger, and your spitting up, none of us got any sleep. This state of affairs, however, did little to lessen our overall euphoria at having you with us. We were the Great Providers, meeting your many needs.

And then it happened. You began to cry.

Your father changed your diaper. You cried. I tried to nurse you, and when that didn't work, I patted you until you burped. You cried. Your father rocked you. I rocked you. And still you cried. Then we got out the "experts"— Spock, Brazelton, and the entire *Princeton Center for Infancy*.

We played quiet music, Brahms and Ravel. We stuck your feet in warm water. We wrapped you in blankets, first tight and then loose. We even tried putting a clock by your head (it works for puppies). Then we rocked you and rocked you and burped you some more. And still, you cried.

It was hard to love you that night. You were no longer the soft, cuddly baby we thought we knew. Your skin was the color of Chicago brick; your body, just as rigid. Your fists jabbed furiously at the air. With eyes squeezed tightly shut, your face was one round screaming mouth. Who is this strange creature, we wondered? Undoubtedly borne by somebody else.

By four in the morning, all three of us were crying. I felt inadequate. Your father felt inadequate. And you, we still didn't know what you were feeling. By the time your father and I dried each other's tears, you were sound asleep.

How many nights like this? Not now, I mean, but in the years to come, when your father and I will hold each other tight as we listen to you crying in another room? Not many, I hope. Few tears are that untouchable.

At these times, however few, we will try our best to let you be, to respect the time you need to find your own peace. But if I should appear at your door with an outstretched hand, a worried look, a plate of cookies, or a candle for the dark, please do not be angry. Try to spare me one moment before you tell me to go. Open your eyes, look at me, and know that *nothing* is the hardest thing for a mother to do.

Mary Knight

What Does Hope Mean to You?

The greatest sight one sees beneath the stars is the sight of worthy motherhood.

George W. Truett

"Better?" I asked, tucking the fresh diaper and returning the baby to his crib in the church nursery where I volunteered. I dreamed of the day—maybe soon—that my husband, Steve, and I would have a little one of our own. But then I spotted my friend Susan, frowning. "I have bad news. Tiffany had her ultrasound. She fell in love with the baby and decided she can't give him up for adoption."

I was happy for the baby; now he'd have the mom that God intended. I also knew how easy it is to fall in love with a blurry ultrasound image, because I'd done it myself, twice.

Only now I'd lost a third baby. *Maybe it will never happen,* I grieved, surrounded by a nursery full of cooing infants. Maybe this is as close as I'll ever get to being a mom.

I lost my first baby at twenty-four weeks. The doctor said we could try again, and the second time I was just as excited, but also terrified.

"Look, you can see the blood pumping through the baby's heart," the doctor reassured me at my thirty-four-week sonogram. But the very next morning I awoke to the same awful stillness. "Not again! What's wrong with me?" I sobbed in the delivery room, a place that's supposed to be filled with the cries of precious newborns.

There were no genetic abnormalities or medical explanations why we'd lost two babies. But I couldn't risk a third. "Our family will have to come a different way," I told Steve, so we had decided to try adoption.

We wrote a letter introducing ourselves and describing our yearning to be parents. "If you know anyone who's pregnant and thinking about adoption, please pass this letter along to them," we asked. My mom and I mailed five hundred copies to friends, church members, even my old babysitters and grammar school teachers.

Someone forwarded our letter to an agency called Loving Option. "We help arrange adoptions," they explained, so Steve and I assembled a scrapbook of photos and family stories to show prospective birth moms.

"My name's Tiffany," the shy, frightened voice on the phone began. She told me how a mutual friend had given her our letter. "I might be able to help you," she said.

I arranged to meet Tiffany at Loving Option. Then our worker called back. "Another birth mom, Brooke, wants to meet you," she said, and my spirits soared because our chances had just doubled.

We met Brooke first, and her three-year-old daughter, Alexis. Alexis spent the whole visit making faces at Steve. "I hate boys," she declared, and by the end of the interview Steve was utterly discouraged: "It's not going to work. Let's hope our meeting with Tiffany goes better."

It did. Tiffany was young and scared, but determined to do what was best for her unborn child. "Do you know if it's a boy or a girl?" I asked.

"I'll tell you next week after my ultrasound," she said, and I was sure she'd choose us.

But after the ultrasound Tiffany decided she couldn't go through with the adoption. *How many more babies can I lose?* I wept, until out of the blue the agency worker called.

"Brooke wants to meet with you again," she said. "Your mom, too, if that's okay."

Steve and I figured Brooke wanted to know who'd be caring for the baby after I returned to work. Mom was happy to go. "For you," she said before the interview, handing me a worry stone that carried a simple inscription: "Hope."

It was like night and day. Instead of making faces at Steve this time, Alexis sat on the floor playing blocks and coloring with him. Brooke and I had a long conversation about life and parenting, and when it was time to go Alexis tapped my leg and said, "My mommy has your baby in her tummy."

No one knew what to say. But a few days later the agency called. "Brooke wants you to come along to her next doctor's visit. She wants you as involved as possible in the birth of your baby."

I went to every appointment. As her due date neared I jumped whenever the phone rang.

Then, on Easter Sunday during church, it rang. "Brooke's on her way to the hospital," Steve said, pocketing his cell. I had to pinch myself: *It's really happening! I'm going to be a mom!*

Brooke insisted Steve and I be in the delivery room. "This is your moment," she said, and I whispered a quick prayer for Brooke because I knew how much it hurt, going into a delivery room and leaving without a baby.

"She's beautiful!" I sighed when Brooke gave birth to a healthy baby girl.

"Would you like to hold her?" the doctor asked Brooke, but she shook her head no.

"Steve and Lori will take good care of her," she said, and handed me a congratulations card she'd brought with her. "I'm so happy I can bless you with the family you've always wanted."

"Hi, Hope, I'm your daddy."

I spent all day racing between the nursery and Brooke's room, wanting to be with them both. "It's going to be tough for her," I said to the Loving Option worker.

"We'll be here for her," she promised. "You and your husband go, now. Enjoy your new family."

We've brought Hope to Loving Option twice for visits with Brooke, and I send letters and photos regularly. I want her to know how much we cherish her precious gift. I also had two paperweights engraved with the definition of the word "Hero"—one for Brooke, the other for Hope, so they'll always have that very special connection.

Maybe one day Steve and I will try again to have a baby, or adopt Hope a little brother or sister. For now I'm enjoying every day changing diapers and rocking Hope to sleep. Our adoption journey has ended, but our life as a family is just beginning.

Lori Fehlinger as told to Heather Black
Previously published in *Women's World* magazine

Because He Loved Me

If I know what love is, it is because of you.

Herman Hesse

Jude had been out of my body for two days. He lay in his little clear plastic "case" next to me, sleeping mostly. I'd often slip my finger into his soft, tiny hand and stare at him when I wasn't entertaining all the visitors we had.

And yet, the crushing bubble was already welling up inside of me, the bubble that would burst soon after I came home. I could feel the pressure of emotions filling up my rib cage. It wasn't just that I felt so fat and so exposed; I felt incapable. I felt more overwhelmed than I'd ever felt about anything—even the cancer I'd dealt with. At least with cancer it was just the disease and me. This time another person was thrown into the mix. A person that I would be responsible for, whose character I would be largely accountable for molding and shaping, who might or might not give me heartfelt Mother's Day cards at some point in his life.

What if I messed it all up? I thought, as a million and one scenarios raced through my mind, which was growing ever manic.

And, as if my mind weren't in enough pain, my body had discovered a whole new level of anguish. I would complain. And then I would feel guilty, because, after all, I did get a baby out of the deal, and women didn't always have it so "easy." And then time would pass and I'd repeat that cycle of complaining and guilt.

So it was on day two, around 7:00 PM, that one of the crabbier nurses on staff came in and announced very flatly that I had to take a shower. *Tonight.* I could sense a hint of disgust in her voice, and I, of course, took that very personally to mean that I especially had to hurry up and shower because of my size.

The bubble of panic inside me grew ever larger.

Chad had just left for the night. My stepmom, Sara, was staying with me that night and letting Chad go home so he could get some real rest. Before I could even think about crying, the tears were streaming down my face. I began to choke back sobs. The nurse looked at me, expressionless, and just left the room.

I knew I couldn't shower by myself. I could barely walk. Someone would have to help me, and I didn't want anyone to see me looking this enormous, swollen, bruised, and disgusting, my lower abdomen stained dark orange from the Betadine covering my C-section incision. I only wanted the help of one person, and he'd just left.

My head was exploding with protests: *I'll just refuse! They can't make me! They can't! I can't let anyone see me like this. I'll die of shame. I'll never stop crying.* And then I remembered that the walk from my hospital room to the parking garage was quite a long one. *Maybe Chad hadn't made it to the car yet. Maybe he'd come back and help me!*

I frantically dialed his cell phone from my hospital line. I could hear the echo of the parking garage in his voice, and he could hear the panic and sorrow in mine. He hadn't left yet and he'd be right back. I was flooded with relief.

I started crying again the minute I saw his face.

Sara said she'd watch the baby while he helped me take my shower.

Chad helped me to the bathroom. I hobbled more with each step, my breath hissing out of me. He helped get my gown off. I grimaced and apologized, but he only shook his head and told me not to worry about anything.

I didn't really want him to have to see me like this, but I couldn't think of anyone else I needed more.

"It's going to be okay," he whispered. "I'm going to help you. Don't worry."

But I worried in spite of myself. I wondered if he'd ever be able to put the horrific picture of what I looked like at that moment out of his mind. I wondered if this moment would forever taint our love life.

He literally had to lift each of my legs into the shower, one at a time, because I was so weak. The warm water felt surprisingly good, but I was terrified of doing anything with my incision. The nurses had told me that I had to directly soap up the stapled gash and softly scrub it with a washcloth. I didn't even want to know how painful that was going to be. I was shaking from weakness and fear.

"Just tell me what to do," he said softly.

And so I guided him. He gently washed my hair first and for a moment, I felt like a little girl again. Then he slowly lathered the rest of my body, avoiding the incision until I was ready.

He was standing outside of the shower and his shirt was soaked.

"You're getting all wet," I said, my voice shaking.

"It's okay. Don't worry about me."

"I guess we need to wash my incision," I said weakly.

Our eyes locked and I began sobbing. I was so afraid and felt so wounded and exhausted. He put his arms around me as I sobbed on his soaking wet shoulder.

"I didn't want you to have to see me like this. I can't believe you have to help me like this. I didn't think that . . ."

"I love you," he said. "You're so beautiful to me. I'd do anything for you. No matter what."

I sobbed even harder. I'd never felt so loved in all my life.

Moments later, he very gently cleaned my incision and surprisingly, the pain was minimal. Then he washed the rest of me. It was something I didn't think a husband should ever have to do, but he did it with such love and compassion. He uttered not one complaint.

He helped me ease out of the shower and wrapped me in a towel. We stood there just holding each other for what seemed like a million years.

I knew having the baby would change our lives forever, but this moment changed our love forever. In those moments, we developed a bond so deep it takes my breath away just thinking about it.

Ginger LeBlanc

Reprinted by permission of Off the Mark and Mark Parisi. © 1994 Mark Parisi.

There's No Place Like Home

For a month before my due date, our apartment looked like the perfect arrangement for the prepared childbirth we had been anticipating. On my husband's night table stood a neat stack of graph paper, each sheet marked off into carefully prepared columns labeled: "Time Beginning," "Time Ending," "Duration of Contraction," and "Interval Between Contractions." A row of sharpened pencils lay beside the papers. On my nightstand could be found an assortment of books on natural childbirth and Lamaze breathing techniques, my bibles all these months. In the hallway stood my packed suitcase for the hospital.

Believing deeply in the value of a natural, drug-free labor and delivery, we had immersed ourselves in classes, readings, and the search for a "believing" obstetrician. We'd been trained to recognize the exact steps labor would take and the techniques for handling each step. Filled with eagerness and confidence, we awaited the opportunity to employ all we had learned, according to plan. Little did we know that Mother Nature does not always operate "by the book," and loves to scoff at human plans.

· One morning, I suddenly awoke at 1:00 AM with a severe stomachache and the urge for a bowel movement. After several trips between bathroom and bed, I decided to time the cramps to see if this could be the beginning of labor.

What I discovered was that the pains were completely irregular in duration as well as spacing, and after several minutes, it was impossible to tell when a pain was ending—the pain was continuous. In addition, the urge to defecate seemed stronger than ever.

If this is labor, I told myself, *then it is not what I had been led to expect. I was supposed to be having evenly spaced contractions, beginning mildly at half-hour intervals, then building in intensity until, hours later, they would be spaced at two-minute intervals.*

I awakened my husband, calmly informing him that this might be the beginning of labor but I was not yet certain. He set himself up with one of his charts, as if ready for a lengthy, leisurely vigil. As I lay in bed, he tried to fit what was tearing me to pieces onto his neat sheets of graph paper. The pattern that emerged was basically what I had experienced earlier—pain was continuous.

At 4:30, my husband wanted to take me to the hospital. I insisted that we still did not know if this was labor or an imminent bowel movement, as the cramps were not following the pattern we'd been taught. I feared that if I did not follow instructions verbatim, emphasized by both doctor and classes, I would panic and then be unable to have the beautiful, natural childbirth I wanted so badly.

The urge to push had become very strong, and in the midst of our discussion about the hospital, I groped my way to the bathroom, confident of a bowel movement and relief this time. My husband announced that he was headed downstairs to bring the car to the front of the building. The thought of being left alone filled me with alarm. My voice, which had been whispery for the previous hour, returned in full force and I heard myself yelling,

"No! Don't leave me here! I'll get dressed and come down with you!"

We argued over the logic of this until I finally settled on asking for my clothes. A few moments later, my husband was pushing my blouse down over my head while I remained on the toilet.

"You can get up now," he said after slipping my feet into a pair of slacks. Two realizations struck: my back was bathed in sweat, and I felt paralyzed and could not move. "Pull me up," I murmured, hugging his waist. As he lifted me up, he suddenly yelled, "Get back to bed, Ruth! The head is coming out!"

Placing my hand lightly on my vagina, I felt a bulging and the top of a little head! Ironically, this lifted the cloud of panic from my chest. I felt joyful and relieved. *So this really is labor after all!* Yet I still refused to face the fact that if the head was crowning, it was the end of labor, not the beginning.

"So now we can go to the hospital," I chirped merrily. My husband stared at me wordlessly, and I knew. There was no time. The baby was to be born here, now, at home. I had been in labor all along, in my sleep as well, and had awakened practically ready to deliver. It had been an unconventional, not "by the book" labor, but labor nonetheless.

In a giddy daze, with my legs spread apart, I slowly made my way to bed. I was calm, floating a thousand feet off the ground. The bedroom took on a new dimension. I noticed the beauty of the early morning light streaming in through the windows. I heard the brash honking of cars in the street below welcoming the new day. I pitied those drivers, those people in the street, as well as everyone just awakening. For them, it would be a normal day, a day like any other. For me, it was to be a magical day of love and triumph.

My husband, meanwhile, was on the phone with the police emergency number, giving our address for an ambulance. He then spoke with a midwife on call. I felt like giggling, but one look at my husband's face told me to stay quiet as he listened intently. *What is he talking about?* I wondered as I heard him telling the midwife that the head was rotating and the shoulders were emerging. I wanted to laugh out loud, in joy and disbelief.

"Don't push now," I was told. I was numb from the waist down, and wondered if Nature was helping me do what was best. My husband then followed the midwife's instructions and put his finger at the side of the baby's neck to check for the umbilical cord. Fortunately, it was not there, which eliminated the necessity of having to slip it off.

As the baby turned, my husband was directed to support its head. With the phone in the crook of his neck, he leaned over and lightly held his hands under the head. The baby—our baby!—let out its first cry, a little peep, and spit up some fluid. "Okay, now you can push," he said when the rotating was completed. I gave a light push, and a tiny child lay in my husband's hands, a little boy!

Noticing the baby opening and then immediately closing one eye, my husband ran to turn off the overhead light as well as the air conditioner. He then grabbed two towels from the closet, wrapped the baby, and gently placed him where he had landed, on the rumpled sheet between my legs. Raising my head to feast my eyes on my sleeping baby boy, I suppressed a choke, certain that my happiness would burst right out of my chest. As my husband continued conversing with the midwife, I admired the most adorable little face and healthy-looking little body.

The apartment was suddenly crowded: a technician who cut the cord and tied a bow on my son's belly button, a policeman who held back shyly at my bedroom door, a policewoman who came charging in and scooped up my baby to cradle him in her arms, and an ambulance driver who maneuvered me into a wheelchair.

They were to take us to the hospital where the baby would be examined, the placenta would be delivered, and I would be stitched. Descending in the quiet, cramped elevator of my apartment building, surrounded by these four strangers, one holding and cooing to my son, I felt certain that the elevator could never travel downward as long as I was flying so high.

Suddenly, in the stillness, the shy policeman asked me my baby's name. Looking up at his friendly, embarrassed face, I nearly choked on the words. "Michael Charles," I stammered. That was the first time I had spoken his name since his birth. Tears streamed down my face. I let them flow, unchecked, and everyone in that elevator was silent.

As the doors opened onto a warm, sunny September morning, I knew that I held something within me now that all the planning and practicing and preparing could not have provided. Wonder for the unexpected in Nature would be a part of me forever, courtesy of my son's magnificent entrance into the world.

Ruth Rotkowitz

Second Fiddle

I think my mother used to like me. It always appeared so. She made such a fuss over my meager accomplishments that no matter what my age, I often felt like a precocious child who had just done or said something quite remarkable.

That is until recently. Until my son was born, to be precise. Until I became the invisible woman, er . . . you know . . . Matthew's mother.

"Oh Matthew's here!" my mother exclaims when he and I arrive for a visit. No "Mary's here" or "Hello, Mary." No greeting for me at all in fact. I'm left standing in the foyer, holding the diaper bag, while my son is whisked off to another room to be entertained by Grandma.

It's no better at my own house.

If my mother's visit happens to coincide with the baby's nap, she doesn't bother to take her coat off. "I'll come back later," she tells me.

Once she returned to find me holding Matthew in one arm and vacuuming with the other. I brightened considerably in anticipation of the kudos I knew I was about to receive. Something along the lines of: "Superwoman entertains an infant and keeps the house spotless simultaneously."

"What are you doing?" she asked accusingly as she grabbed the baby from my arms. "Poor Matthew, poor baby," she soothed sweetly, looking up occasionally to glare in my direction.

Poor Matthew? What about poor daughter? I wondered.

Apparently she's been supplanted by "poor grandson."

The other day I called my mother on the telephone. My voice was hoarse and rasping.

"Do you have a cold?" she asked anxiously.

"Yes, I feel terrible," I began woefully, ready to unleash a long list of sorry symptoms in an effort to gain some sympathy, and possibly some homemade chicken soup.

She cut me short.

"Don't go near the baby," was all she offered.

When I pointed out that it would be next to impossible for me to avoid contact with my infant son, my mother reconsidered.

"Then wear a surgical mask," she ordered.

I laughed.

Two hours later she arrived with a dozen of them.

I don't know why all of this surprises me. One month after Matthew was born, I caught my mother replacing all of the pictures in her wallet.

Discarded on the kitchen table were Mary's baby picture, Mary's first day of school, Mary's graduation from elementary school, high school, and college, and Mary's wedding picture.

In their place went Matthew's hospital picture, Matthew coming home from the hospital, Matthew in his bassinet, and Matthew being fed.

"Don't you have room for even one picture of me?" I asked.

She considered this.

"You know, you're right," she said finally. "I should include one picture of Matthew with his mother."

Mary Vallo

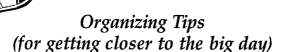

Organizing Tips
(for getting closer to the big day)

- Consider labeling drawers and closet shelves by contents. For example, use labels for the onesies, pajamas, baby outfits, receiving blankets, burp cloths, socks, sweaters, and so on. This helps when your spouse takes a turn changing the baby or when you have family members and friends come over to help out.

- Keep key items ready in the most used rooms of the house: burp cloths, blankets, tissues, antibacterial solution, and hand lotion (for dry hands caused by frequent hand washing).

- If you live in a large home, it might be helpful to have two "baby-changing stations" for the first few months—one in the baby's room and another in the main room of the house where you spend most of your time. For the second "station," just a changing diaper pad on a counter with the necessities nearby would do the trick.

3

A SHOULDER
TO LEAN ON

*There is . . . nothing to suggest that mothering
cannot be shared by several people.*

H. R. Schaffer

It's Not a Piece of Cake

If evolution really works, how come mothers only have two hands?

Ed Dussault

My first child was less than a month old the day that I leaned limp and crying against the front door. The salesperson knocking on the other side of it must have heard the hysterical shrieking coming from the crib, but I refused to answer. I could feel my confidence crumbling amid shattered expectations and wished fervently that my mother would somehow read my muddled mind and come to my rescue.

Throughout my childhood my mother had fit the mold by being everything that everyone expected of her. She was disciplined and organized in a way that I would never come to understand in the time that I was living under her roof. Nor did I ever truly comprehend the level of competence and responsibility with which she faced each aspect of her life.

In my own first days of motherhood, I would come to resent that competence. It's not that she wouldn't have come if I had called. A woman who had always made time for me, she would have dropped her current activity and arrived with record promptness. She would have come bearing food and cleaning supplies and a shoulder to cry on. She would have been the pillar of strength and security that compensated for my own inadequacies. If only I could have dredged up my own inner power and matched her practiced efficiency.

As the tears dried on my tired cheeks and I watched the baby finally sleeping, unbidden bitterness crept in. *How dare she let me grow up with the misconception that being a mom was a piece of cake? With what delusion had I decided that I could tackle the endless demands of homemaking, pregnancy-induced bodily changes, and the adjustment to new motherhood? Whose wisdom had I subjected myself to that had resulted in a situation for which I was clearly not designed? And why, when I had been successful at so many other ventures, did I have to be a failure at the one thing that meant the most to me?*

The morning came when I did make the call. The gloom that was covering my home was becoming too thick to see through, and the tears were flowing too freely for reason. When the last of the dishes were put away and the worst of the laundry taken care of, I faced my mother with the questions that had plagued me. Why had she made it look so easy, so that I was completely unequipped for the reality of motherhood? When violent mood swings warred with sheer exhaustion, my mind had screamed in outrage at the image of her keeping her door frames dutifully dusted when I could barely find the energy to pick matching socks.

Etched in my memory forever is the sad smile that filled her bewildered face and the words that would change my perspective forever. Sitting comfortably with a warm mug in hand, she reached across to hold my shaky fingers and reminded me of the moments in my childhood when she had lost her temper with me. We reminisced about the times that the house had not been spotless, when the meal had burned, or the laundry had gotten behind. And I began to remember the mornings when we had been late getting up, and the days when we had lost something valuable or forgotten something important or endured a great disappointment. And she confided that there had been moments of sadness, of frustration, of feeling overwhelmed.

My eyes filled with familiar tears. "Why," I asked, "if you had experienced these same difficult times, had I never known it? Why did I grow up believing that you lived in some kind of enviable bliss?"

She met my confused expression with rueful eyes. "Because above all else," she answered, "it was important to ensure that my child grow up knowing unconditional love, untainted by moments of anger or distress. I had to make my child feel cherished," she said, "and not reminded of those inconveniences you innocently caused."

That afternoon, in my small dusty home, I became acquainted with my mother, the woman. Two generations saw each other with impeccable clarity for one timeless instant. The moment was healing.

SG Birch

Needing More than Groceries

Tears are the safety valve of the heart when too much pressure is laid on.

Albert Smith

This was my first outing as a mother of two, and I'd prepared for it like a climber preparing to conquer Mount Everest. The diaper bag was loaded with colic medicine, breast pads, wipes, diapers in two sizes, little containers of Cheerios—anything and everything I thought I might need for an hour away with a newborn and a twenty-month-old. I was ready. At least I hoped I was. I strapped both girls in their car seats, took a deep breath, and got behind the wheel for the first time in three weeks. *I can do this,* I thought.

The first few minutes went well. Molly slept in her carrier nestled in the shopping cart. Not much room for groceries, but that couldn't be helped. As I lifted Haley up into the cart, I smelled a familiar odor. "Poo Poo," she crooned proudly. *No kidding.* "There's a changing table in the ladies' room at the far end of the store," a clerk informed me. I headed that way.

As we walked, shopper after shopper stopped to admire baby Molly, completely ignoring Haley. Haley squirmed and twisted around in the seat trying to get their attention. When this didn't work she grabbed a roll of paper towels off the shelf and dropped it on Molly's head. Molly wailed and in my sleep-deprived state I started crying too. We were barely inside the front door. I hadn't placed a single thing in the cart. This was not looking good. I scrambled to unstrap Molly from her carrier. Haley started crying too. The second I picked Molly up, my breasts took it as their cue and started gushing. The breast pads packed neatly in the diaper bag did me no good. The front of my blouse was soaked in seconds. Seeing me hold Molly, Haley started screaming, "I wanna get down! I wanna get down." I felt like everyone was looking at me and thought of making a dash for the parking lot. *Maybe we can eat next week.* With my free hand, I lifted Haley out of the cart. As soon as her feet hit the floor, she took off running down the aisle and out of sight.

What a spectacle I must have been scrambling after her, a squalling baby in my arms, tears streaming down my face, my blouse soaked with breast milk. *I was wrong,* I thought. *I can't do this.* All I wanted to do was take my two babies home, crawl under the covers, and never venture out again. I caught up with Haley two aisles away and sat down on the floor beside her, exhausted and defeated.

Other shoppers passed. A mom with older kids half smiled. Another looked at me then turned and walked the other way. I felt like I hadn't slept in months and thought, *Surely they remember what this is like.* I thought of my sisters who have four and five kids each. They make it look so easy. I bet they never fell to pieces on the floor of the dog food aisle. I mustered what strength I had and got back to my feet. From somewhere in my cobwebby mind came an old trick of my mom's. I started singing, "We're almost

finished. Then we're going home. Haley is a good girl."
Haley stopped crying, more surprised than consoled. I
coaxed her back to the cart, propped Molly on one shoulder, and opened a box of raisins. I remembered something
from my parenting books and started talking to Haley
about what we'd do when we got home. She walked along
beside the cart munching her raisins and listening,
appeased for the moment. I considered whether to go on
or just admit I was defeated and go home.

As I resumed the search for the restroom, still singing
feebly, another shopper passed, a woman about ten years
older than I, dressed in a stylish business suit and sporting a perfect manicure. I felt like a slug. She smiled as she
passed and said, "Those are two lucky little girls." I can't
tell you how her words bolstered me. They felt like a shot
of vitamins and a good night's sleep all in one. *She's right,*
I thought. *I'm doing the best I can. I'm a good mother!* Just to
know that someone understood how tired I was, maybe
that's all I needed. In six words she'd said so much. She'd
given me permission to be human, to stop trying to be
supermom, and to stop beating myself up when I couldn't
do it. She knew I didn't have a clue how to pull this off,
but in her few words and with her smile she'd said that
she'd been where I was and survived. She knew I could
do it, too. We were sisters in this sacred vocation called
motherhood.

I won't say the next two hours were easy. We made
three trips to the restroom for diaper changes and one
more to breast-feed Molly. The ice cream melted before we
got to the checkout. Haley cried a few more times, and I
pulled Mama's singing trick to calm us both. But I managed to buy most of what I set out for, and when we got
home we all took a nice, long nap.

I wish I knew who that thoughtful shopper was. I wish
I could thank her for reaching out to a tired, overwhelmed,

insecure new mom, for saying just the words I needed to hear when I needed to hear them most.

I'm shopping with four kids now, and I still have days when I wonder if I can put one foot in front of the other. But more often I find myself looking for another tired mom in the store, the doctor's office, the dry cleaner who just needs to hear that she's not alone, that someone understands how tired and overwhelmed she feels. I try to give her permission to be human. Who knows? Today it might be me providing that much-needed lift for someone else.

Mimi Greenwood Knight

The Good Doctor

When I became a new mom, I was as lost as a tiny baby myself. Hold her, burp her, feed her . . . I had no idea how to do anything! I probably still wouldn't know what I was doing if it wasn't for Dr. Shemesh.

The day we took little Katie home from the hospital, my husband, Mike, and I buckled her into the brand-new Fisher-Price car seat, adjusted her little pink bonnet, and drove home. *Now what?*

We bumbled through the feedings and changings and long sleepless nights. At last it was time for our first visit to the pediatrician. Dr. Lorit Shemesh hadn't been difficult to select—she was the only pediatrician for miles around. I hoped she'd be able to tell us everything we needed to know. We entered the tidy little waiting room, armed with a page-long typed list of questions.

The first thing Dr. Shemesh did was to take Katie from my arms and hold her close, her long, delicate fingers gently wrapping around Katie's tiny bottom. The doctor looked directly in Katie's eyes and spoke to her. "Ah, you're doing just fine. What a good, strong girl." She praised everything from the sparse tufts of bright red hair to the ten little toes, making us feel they were the best baby toes she'd ever seen. Katie responded by reaching up and grasping a hank of the doctor's shiny black hair.

I watched carefully while Dr. Shemesh weighed, measured, and poked. Everything seemed fine, but that didn't calm my anxious heart. We produced our list and fired away. How could we be sure she was getting enough milk? Was it best to bathe her in the morning or evening? How could we keep her safe from germs? Dr. Shemesh patiently answered everything.

"Doctor, she cries an awful lot," I reported.

"Yes." Dr. Shemesh nodded. "Babies cry a lot."

"And during the day, she sleeps an awful lot. Is she sleeping enough? Or too much?"

"New babies need a lot of rest."

Finally, the *real* question came out. "But are we doing everything right? What are we supposed to be doing with her?" I blurted. I wanted everything to be just right.

A gentle smile spread across Dr. Shemesh's face. "Just talk to her. Read to her. Show her things." Then she paused before adding, "Know what a baby needs most? Lots of love."

Our sweet little girl cooed softly. Already I felt a deep, warm bond.

We managed to relax a bit and get the hang of bathing and diapering and feeding. Whenever we were unsure, we'd call the doctor's office for advice. Dr. Shemesh would return the call right away. "Did you try burping her?" she'd say. "It's probably gas." Or, "It sounds like an ear infection. Come on over, I'll squeeze you in." Often, she'd call back in the evening after the office closed. "How is Katie feeling now? What is her temperature?" Although we worried about disturbing the doctor, she always encouraged us to call, no matter the hour.

But what Dr. Shemesh taught us most was not about medicine.

One day we were pushing Katie in a cart in the grocery store when we spotted Dr. Shemesh in the produce aisle. She was shopping for her husband, who was also a busy doctor, and their children. Surely she had many things to do, yet she abandoned her basket and approached our cart.

"My, my, Katie," she said, lifting her out of the infant seat. "How are we today?" I was used to keeping my baby close by my side, so at first I felt a little anxious when the doctor took her. She walked off, traipsing Katie up and down the produce aisle. "Look, Katie," she picked up a bright, round fruit from the display. "Lemon." She held the lemon close to Katie's eyes. Katie batted at the fruit with her tiny fists. "Rough. Bumpy. Yellow," Dr. Shemesh explained. Next, she showed her an orange. Katie responded, her big blue eyes shining with interest. After a few moments, the doctor returned Katie to her seat. She didn't have to say a word to me, but from her example I learned how to explore the world with my child and foster her natural curiosity.

Although most of her advice was well received, there actually was some advice we never tried. When Katie was about six months old, she had no interest in solid food. She was gaining weight satisfactorily, but still I worried. "Try gefilte fish," Dr. Shemesh suggested, referring to a popular ethnic food. "It's tender and tastes great. She'll love it." But that jar of honeycombed slabs of white fish didn't look too appetizing to me. Dr. Shemesh offered another suggestion. "I'll take her home for the weekend," she offered. "I'll get her to eat." I knew that the doctor was serious. I knew that she wouldn't charge me for it either. But I couldn't imagine parting with my baby for a whole weekend. Finally, the doctor's most helpful advice did the trick. "Don't worry. She'll eat when she's ready." And she did.

Years later, when Dr. Shemesh decided she needed to take a few years off practice to spend some time with her family, she called each parent personally to explain. Although I miss her loving guidance terribly, I know she gave me the most invaluable gift. She was brilliant in the field of medicine, but she also knew a lot about life. She taught me everything I needed to know about being a parent. When I was striving to do everything right, she taught me the most right thing I could do was to just love my child.

Peggy Frezon

The Second Greatest Gift

You never know what gifts you will receive in your lifetime, but the best gifts come when you least expect them.

I had the difficult situation of being a married, single mom for the first year and a half of my son's life. My husband, a member of the California Army National Guard, was deployed to Iraq just three weeks after Mason was born.

Having a new baby is one thing for a young couple and quite another for a single person. We made it home from the hospital in time to get settled in with our baby. Shortly thereafter, we started packing and preparing to see Dave off to war.

With Dave gone, life with just Mason and me was quiet and somewhat routine. I read all the books and consulted both grandmas, learning that having your newborn baby on a schedule was the way to go. Unfortunately, Mason decided to create his own schedule; he slept most of the day and wanted to eat most of the night. Mind you, he did plenty of eating throughout the day, but he did not miss that two-hour mark during the sleeping hours of the night either. I fielded phone calls from friends and family wanting to know how we were getting along and wishing us well. Every call that came in brought some sort of "good" advice about how to get Mason to sleep more during the night.

It wasn't long until my days and nights were running together and I found odd things going on in my normally organized household. There were frozen peas in the refrigerator, not frozen anymore. There were pillows on the bed without pillowcases . . . for weeks at a time.

But my favorite was the night I went to a Christmas party dinner. I had Mason in his carrier on the floor next to my chair. He was starting to doze off as the salad was being served. I glanced down at him and then at my watch, realizing that I might only have ten minutes to eat before I had to tend to him.

I was really hungry and excited by the thought that I might get to eat a full meal with real silverware, while sitting in a chair. As I ate the salad, I tasted the greens, the tomato, the onion, and the garlic flavor of the croutons. I thought about what might be for dinner and hoped it would arrive before Mason stirred. As I started to put the last forkful of salad in my mouth, a very nice man sitting next to me leaned over with a boat of salad dressing and asked if I would like some on my salad, which was now all gone. I was so excited to eat a real meal—not leftovers, eaten with my fingers in thirty seconds while leaning over the kitchen sink—that I did not even realize that the salad had no dressing on it!

The following day, one of my very dearest friends called and asked how we were doing. I am not sure what I said to her, but her response was that she would be over the day after tomorrow to see Mason and me.

Sure enough, two days (or were they nights?) went by and here was Dahlynn at my door, with an overnight bag. She came in and informed me that she had come to spend the night with Mason so I could sleep. Like a pro (well, she does have two children of her own), Dahlynn assessed the situation, recognized the sleep deprivation, and was on the job. She fed Mason *and* me, then, even though I protested, feeling like I had to show her *this* and help her do *that*, she ran me out of the kitchen and into the bathroom to enjoy a bath. I took a long, hot bubble bath and then, completely exhausted, I went to bed. In bed, I wondered if Dahlynn was thinking that my house was a disaster and if Mason was okay with her and not with me . . . zzzzzzzz.

I woke up the next day a little dazed and confused. My eyelids were stuck together and my mouth was dry from rich, deep sleep. The sun was shining, and I was in my bed, clean, with actual pillowcases on my pillows! I smelled coffee and heard giggles and cooing in the kitchen . . . was I in heaven? With a big smile, I knew I was not in heaven. I realized that I had just received my second greatest gift, next to Mason—a good, full night's sleep from my dear, sweet angel of a friend.

Kathleen Partak

What Every New Mom Really Needs . . . the Gift of Experience

I remember how thrilled I was with the pale yellow layettes and darling crocheted blankets I received at my first baby shower. Indeed, I think I wrinkled my nose at the more practical gifts of diaper rash cream and baby clippers and wondered why the gift-givers were not more gracious and creative. What I really loved best in my pre-parent naïveté was the white smocked dress . . . size 12 months.

Ha! That outfit was worn exactly one time before it was permanently stained with something very sticky and pinkish. The pale yellow layettes were newborn-sized and only fit my full-term baby for a week or so tops. At that same shower I think we received about three dozen stuffed animals. One tiny teddy bear was the baby's favorite from the get-go and all the rest languished in a big, dusty pile. I alternately shoved them from a basket to a hammock to a plastic container tucked into the closet. They finally disappeared to my great relief at a yard sale the year the baby turned five.

Now that I've done the whole baby thing five times

over the course of just over a decade, I think I am pretty qualified to put together a new mom survival kit. Trust me when I tell you to take this kit to your next baby shower. The recipient may wrinkle her nose a bit at your lack of white eyelet or lace bonnets. But, believe me, she'll thank you when she's six or nine months into her adventure and she realizes that yours is the gift she has reached for every day. Those little smocked dresses will still be hanging in the closet waiting for picture day, but your basket will be at her side 24/7.

So grab this list and head to the store. No, not the baby superstore. These gifts are for the mom. Who ever said all the good stuff has to go to the baby? If she's a first-time mom she has no idea how much attention she is about to lose just as soon as she gives birth. Forevermore she will be in the wings, completely off center stage. So give her a gift that lets her know you're thinking of her in a big way.

First stop, the pain reliever aisle. Grab the hugest bottle of ibuprofen you can find. It will come in handy for those days immediately following the birth, the months after if she's breast-feeding, and the years after as the child learns to walk, talk, and argue. You might want to buy her a case.

Next, stock up on her caffeinated drink of choice. Perhaps she was a good pregnant person and gave up caffeine while she was expecting. Perhaps she plans to continue without it if she's breast-feeding. Whatever. Sooner or later she is going to need a shot of some sort of stimulant just to stay awake until 6:00 PM.

Stroll on over to the makeup counter and get her some really good under-eye concealer. She's probably expecting to be up a little bit until the baby sleeps through the night. But she has no idea what toll this will take on her face. Or the fact that babies start sleeping through the night only to start teething and/or suffer their first cold.

Moving on, grab the biggest package of paper plates

you can find. Commonly referred to in my house as "the family china pattern," they are among the most wonderful inventions for mothers ever. This is another gift that will last throughout her newborn's childhood. The busy days of infancy when there's just not time to do the dishes . . . the crazy days of toddlerhood when the precious darling likes to throw the plates on the floor . . . and the whirlwind days of adolescence when they're eating fourteen times per day and like to grab a new dish for each refill.

Next on the list are kneepads. I'll never forget the surprise I felt when I noticed I'd worn a hole in the knees of my favorite jeans. I couldn't imagine how it had happened until it dawned on me that I spend an amazing amount of time each day on the floor. I tie shoes, scrub sticky spots, bathe little people, wrestle, play card games, fold clothes . . . and that's just on Monday.

If you are really a good friend, you will invest in a white-noise machine for the mom-to-be. I finally got one of these and felt like a prisoner freed since I no longer had to tip-toe around during naptime or sit six inches from the TV to hear it in the evening after bedtime. I could even keep the phone ringer on and not cringe each time the doorbell rang.

Last but not least you need to get the biggest box of tissues you can find. These are right up there with paper plates on the list of great inventions. Sure, they wipe snotty noses and clean up drool. They're good for picking up unidentified gooey stuff and for stuffing into the pockets of sniffly kids. But perhaps what they're best for is drying tears. And that new mom has no idea how many tears she has ahead of her. Some from pain, a lot from joy, and a few from realizing her favorite jeans are ruined.

Susanna Hickman Bartee

The Perfect Recording

The love of our neighbor in all its fullness simply means being able to say, "What are you going through?"

Simone Weil

Summer had dropped on Missouri like a bomb, so I decided to take my baby daughter, Rhianna, for her first dip in the pool. It wasn't an easy task: with my husband living over a thousand miles away, I'd have to single-handedly entertain her for the hour it took me to blow up the PVC baby boat, maneuver my daughter's stroller out of the car, and open it with one hand while I held her in the other. Still, stroller, float, baby, mother, and camcorder all successfully visited the pool at the edge of our apartment complex, and that day, if you'd asked me, I would have said we had a great time.

A couple of weeks later, as I watched the home video I'd taken, the images seemed to say differently. Since I'd had to film it myself, tossing the camera aside a few times to steady Rhianna in her teetering baby boat, much of the video consisted of wild scans of sky and upside-down apartment buildings. There was almost no commentary, because I'd felt silly talking to myself at the pool, and the little bit of uninterrupted video I had gotten was an extreme close-up of half of Rhianna's face with my left hand in the foreground balancing the boat. The video seemed, to me, to tell the empty little story of life as a semi-single mom.

It was also, I thought, an accurate depiction of how incomplete a job I was doing at motherhood. The week before my daughter was born, we'd moved across the country to a new town where I had no family or friends. My daughter was born via emergency C-section that August 24; on September 1 my husband left me to start his own new job on the East Coast. I had to leave my daughter at day care and start my own new gig when she was only six weeks old. Other single mothers I knew at least had family or friends around to spell them. The only release I got that fall was during my daily stroller walk with her around our apartment complex, when we both took in the fresh air and watched our neighbors walk their puppies and play with their small children. But as the October winds blew in and the snow came, even that would eventually fall by the wayside. "I don't know how you do it," I heard over and over again from well-meaning neighbors and strangers.

They didn't know that I wasn't "doing it." My apartment was always a mess. I prepared my classes five minutes before I taught them. Desperate as I was to make friends, I passed up social invitations because I was so exhausted. I barely had time to record my daughter's "firsts." I scribbled a hurried note on a scrap of paper only to forget what "3/12/05—turned other side" meant. And after hauling a newborn around all day when I still wasn't able to bend at the waist, I fell into bed exhausted and demoralized.

Worst of all, I felt that Rhianna was missing out on so

much by having to be the child of a woman in such a lonely situation. When she fell ill with pneumonia, I had to take her out in subzero weather at three in the morning because I had no one to keep her at home while I went to the pharmacy. I couldn't videotape her first swing at the park because I was the one swinging her. Sometimes I worried, *with no one around to record little things like that, who but me would ever see her infancy? Who would see the pure pleasure on her face as I squirted her with her bath toys? Who would see how she giggled as I tickled her belly?* Faced with the prospect of spending my first Mother's Day at home alone, I took her out for a walk in the stroller. After a hard, icy winter, I thought that a walk on a nice May day might keep me from bursting into tears.

And that's when it happened. One of my neighbors approached us, a young man I'd never before noticed. "Look at her! I remember when she was just an itty-bitty thing and you used to walk her around. Hi sweetie," he said to my daughter. And then, "She's beautiful."

Rhianna, a budding ham, turned and smiled at me. And that's when I realized that through the winter, we hadn't been alone. There had been the bag boys at the grocery who bent over and played with my daughter every time we went shopping, the day care teacher who never failed to comment on how much Rhianna was growing, the young nurse who'd brought me coffee the night I went to the ER with my daughter. In fact, we'd had a lot of help, a lot of moral support. My daughter was not an unhappy baby. Here she was, now, toothlessly grinning at me. And you know what? It wasn't on videotape, and yet I'd always remember that smile, more clearly than if I'd burned it onto a thousand DVDs. That smile would never be for anyone but me. And that's what made it so precious.

Jacinda Townsend

The Bliss of Motherhood

I dreamed of being a mother ever since I was a child. When my husband and I got engaged one of the first things I said was, "We'll be parents!" Even before I got pregnant I pored over parenting magazines reading the articles about each blissful moment. I learned about the art of playing make-believe with my child, hundreds of ideas for healthy snacks, and bedtime stories that really put a child to sleep. All the mothers in the photos looked happy; of course they were, they were mothers!

My best friend, Adriana, was pregnant before I was, and as we marveled at her swelling belly, we discussed and debated issues such as cloth diapers versus disposable, nighttime nursing, immunizations, and the family bed. We took long walks and whispered about the bedraggled mothers we saw who had "let themselves go." We swore we would never let that happen to us. After she gave birth I became pregnant, and though I was queasy for almost the whole term, I was overjoyed and already in love with the growing baby inside me.

During my pregnancy I was surprised and disappointed at the distance I felt from Adriana. Her new baby was strong and healthy, growing beautifully, but Adriana wasn't glowing the way I expected her to. She didn't have as much time for me as I wanted; her son needed naps, feedings, changing. If I went to her house it took her so long to get out the door with him to join me on a walk, and even then our conversations were constantly interrupted as her son needed her attention, again. And all she had to talk about was how tired she was. I was tired too! My big belly made sleeping almost impossible. But if I tried to talk about my tiredness, she just looked at me, shook her head, and said, "Honey, you have no idea what tired really is." *Where was my friend who laughed with me until the wee hours of the morning?* She seemed distracted and lost. *Is this where I was headed? Not if I could help it. But would I be able to help it?*

When my daughter was born I was shocked both at her beauty and at the enormity of love that poured through me for her. That profound feeling of love was a gift beyond imagination.

When Adriana came to bring us dinner shortly after the birth, we marveled together at these new, tender lives that we were capable of creating and sustaining. I thought maybe our friendship could bloom again now that we were both mothers, yet I had little time for visits. The pace of my days was confusing to me; everything had slowed way down, yet I couldn't keep up with anything. Nothing was linear anymore; I had to drop whatever I was doing, constantly, and tend to the little one. I was exhausted.

One night my baby cried inconsolably. Her father and I took turns walking her and singing, as nursing was not what she wanted. Finally, just as it was getting light outside, she fell asleep. Later that morning I sacrificed letting her scream in exchange for taking more than a one-minute shower. I actually washed my hair. "It's okay, sweetie!" I called to her, over and over, as I hastily scrubbed my head, forgoing the conditioner. I dressed quickly and settled her for a feeding, anxiously watching the clock as I didn't want us to be late for her two-week doctor's appointment. *She's happy, she's relaxed,* I thought. *I don't want to stop her from nursing. And she needs to be changed. And the diaper bag needs to be restocked. We're going to be late.*

At the doctor's appointment I was almost in tears as I explained the horrible night we had just had. "What could be wrong with her?" The doctor looked at me with kindness, and said, "Nothing's wrong. It's called a hard night. There will be more of those, I assure you. She's as healthy and normal as can be."

On the way home I saw an old friend, who was not yet a mother, at the grocery store. Having known me for a long time she knew of my yearning for a child. She took a good long look at the blue eyes of my beautiful baby and said with a big smile, "So are you totally blissed-out all the time?"

"Uh, sure, of course I am," I replied, as I clumsily placed my purchases on the counter while balancing a tender bundle of baby. But as I drove home I knew I had not told the truth. I wondered what was wrong with me. *Shouldn't I be happier than I felt? Didn't I have everything I always wanted?* When I took my baby out of the car I looked deeply at her perfect round face, her little pink mouth, and her blue eyes. I was shocked, again, at the surge of intense love that I felt for this tiny being. Yet I was in tears as I carried her and the groceries into the house.

That night, as my husband was cleaning up dinner, I lay in our bed nursing the baby and reading the mothering magazines that used to bring me such pleasure. Lately, when I picked up a magazine and read stories and articles about the joys of parenting, I felt guilty, like I must be doing it wrong, and tears would spring from my eyes.

Reading the letter section of one magazine, I suddenly became riveted. Here was a mother speaking out strongly to the editors. "Contrary to what you would like us to believe, being a new mother is not completely blissful," she wrote. "I have never loved this way in my life, and I have never hurt this much in my life, and I feel betrayed that everybody paints the portrait of motherhood in only pink and blue. There are times when I am so sleep deprived I feel that I can't do this anymore—but I have to. I feel like a monster for being so angry and sad and crazy in the presence of my perfect baby. No one prepared me for the depth of this sacrifice. My world has been blown open, and I stand here in the rawness and allow it for the sake of my baby—anything for the sake of my baby. New mothers need support from each other, but first we have to be willing to tell the truth, the intense, painful, exhausting, milky, poopy, messy truth."

My face was now wet. Sobs poured through me, sobs that had needed to come for two weeks. *This is really hard and I'm not alone in knowing this,* I thought. *Someone else has spoken the truth for me. Who was she? I wanted to send her a note of gratitude.* The letter continued to the next page, where it ended with a name, town, and state. I was now laughing through my tears as I picked up the phone.

"Adriana," I said as I wept, "I just read your letter in the magazine. I had no idea."

Both of us cried, each with a baby at our breast, as we revealed truth after truth about the hardness, the darkness. We began a lifelong process of clearing ourselves out, making more room for the brilliance of our love to shine forth for our children, for our friendship, and for other mothers who are ready to speak the whole truth.

Lava Mueller

Reprinted by permission of Off the Mark and Mark Parisi. © 1997 Mark Parisi.

A Friend in Need Is Family Indeed

*She never quite leaves her children at home,
even when she doesn't take them along.*

Margaret Culkin Banning

I dragged myself up the steps and headed for the nursery. "I'm coming, sweetie." My six-month-old son was crying at the top of his lungs. *Again!* I felt like crying too. I
loved him with all my heart, and it frustrated me that I
couldn't do anything for him. And I didn't have anyone to
turn to. My husband had received a promotion and we'd
left our families to move from the Midwest to New York
right after I learned I was pregnant.

I'd expected my firstborn to be the perfect Gerber baby
in every way. And he was, except for the crying. The
pediatrician said that Christopher was colicky, but he'd
eventually outgrow it.

"In the meantime, this new formula should help relieve
some of his gas," he said.

I'd fed my cranky boy his bottle with the prescribed formula, but it didn't help. Neither did wrapping him snugly
in his favorite blanket or rocking him. I even tried warm

baths, with soft lighting and quiet music in the background. Nothing helped. My son continued to wail as I patted his back. "C'mon, burp honey," I pleaded. I was so discouraged I wanted to run away.

Hey, maybe we both need to get away?

"Come on champ, we're going to go out." I thought that a nice walk in the sunshine just might do the trick. I dressed Chris in a dapper little sailor outfit, complete with a navy blue beret. I scooped him up, kissing his tear-stained face. "Let's go, sweetie." I buckled him into his stroller and pushed him down the block. By the time we reached the end of the street he was quiet. I stopped for a second to check; sure enough, his eyes were closed, his chin drooped onto his little chest.

"Hey Sue," my neighbor Diane waved from her porch. "How about a cup of coffee?"

"Sorry, I can't stop or Christopher might wake up."

"Hold up, I'll put Amy in her stroller and walk with you."

I kept moving up and down the block until she joined me.

"Gee, Sue, not to hurt your feelings, but you look beat," Diane said as she walked beside me.

"I know. Chris is still colicky, and we're not getting much sleep. The new formula the pediatrician prescribed didn't work. He told me to hang in there, that he'll outgrow it."

"Easy for him to say," Diane said. "Now that Amy's two, things are pretty easy, but back when she was an infant, I had my hands full too."

"Yeah, waaahh, I want my mommy," I teased. But I meant it, I felt so alone with no family around.

"Sue," Diane said as we reached her house, "let me take Chris for the afternoon. You need a break."

"Well," I hesitated, "that's nice, but you may regret offering. He cries a lot."

"Let me worry about that. Just bring me his diaper bag; I'll take care of the rest."

I ran the bag over to her house, crammed with bottles, diapers, rattles, and teething biscuits. Plans to catch up with the cleaning crowded my mind. It was exhilarating to think of a neat, orderly house again. Maybe I'd even prepare a real dinner for a change.

I got home and rolled up my sleeves. No sooner had I hauled out the cleaning supplies and the vacuum when the phone rang.

"Hey, I forgot to tell you. My offer to take care of Christopher was conditional. I see you over there getting ready to clean."

I looked out my sliding glass doors and saw Diane standing at her front door. She waved.

"Yeah, my house is a wreck, and I figured I'd catch up on my cleaning."

"No, this day is for you. Read, nap, or soak in a bubble bath, whatever you want to do to relax—no chores. If I see you working, I'm bringing Chris right home. Now, pamper yourself, and that's an order," Diane said sternly. Then her voice softened. "You need this, Sue."

Guess I had to play it her way. I went upstairs and filled the tub with hot water, adding a generous helping of bubble bath. I put Kenny G on in the background and even lit some candles.

Easing myself into the luxuriously scented water, I closed my eyes and leaned my head back. Ah, sweet peace and quiet.

When I woke up, the water had grown cold. I hopped out of the tub and toweled off, feeling refreshed. I smiled as I slipped into a nice outfit and even slathered on some lip gloss and mascara.

What should I do, read a chapter of my new book or call my mom? I couldn't decide.

Who was I kidding? I missed my baby. Sure, the break was nice, but I wanted my boy in my arms.

Sheepishly, I crossed the street and rapped on Diane's door. She'd think I was nuts coming for my son after only two short hours.

"I was wondering when you'd be here to get Chris. I knew you'd miss him," she said placing him in my arms.

"Yep, I did," I admitted as I hugged him. "But the break was sure delicious. Thanks, Di. If you ever need me to watch Amy, I'm just across the street."

I took Chris home that day, and he cried through most of it and for a couple of months more after that. But he did outgrow it. Until then Diane was right there for me, a new mom, all alone in a strange place. She calmed my fears and dried my tears and always seemed to call or drop by at the exact right moment. She'll probably never know what she did for me, or that I didn't really consider her a neighbor at all. She was family. And having family there for me helped me be the best new mom I could ever be.

Susan A. Karas

Mom Friends: Why You Need Them

Sometimes the laughter in mothering is the recognition of the ironies and absurdities. Sometimes, though, it's just pure, unthinkable delight.

Barbara Schapiro

I once heard someone say, "There's no one lonelier than a new mother." I can attest to that. I knew I was in trouble the day I found myself out in the driveway cornering the meter reader, subjecting him to every detail of my daughter's birth. The poor man had a schedule to keep, and I knew I had to let him go. But I was starved for adult company, intelligent conversation.

How had I gone from an advertising executive with an exciting career and a busy social life to someone who saw the high point of her life as collecting enough diaper coupons to send away for the free tote bag? A few short months earlier, I had everything I'd ever wanted. My husband, David, and I were starting our family late, after pinching pennies for years so I could afford to be a full-time mom. Now, our first child was on the way, I'd put in my notice at work, aced my Lamaze class, and the nursery was ready for action.

Then, Haley made her entrance, a month early, via emergency C-section—no Lamaze. That was the first indication that my expectations weren't realistic. The next indication came just a few hours after the birth of my beautiful daughter. I can only imagine how pitiful I looked wandering the halls of the maternity ward, my belly in the lead, portable IV in tow. I was a woman on a mission! An older lady passed and smiled, "Don't worry, hon. You'll have that baby any minute."

She was gone before I managed, "But, I had her yesterday!" It was true. I didn't look much different from when I checked into the hospital, but that was just fluid, right?

I finally found what I'd been hunting: a scale! Gingerly I hoisted up one foot, then the other. My eyes were fixed on the numbers in front of me as I inched the metal weights from left to right and stared in horror! I tried again with the same result. Was this somebody's idea of a joke? I delivered an eight-pound baby sixteen hours ago. Shouldn't I have lost at least, well, eight pounds? Why didn't anybody tell me about this?

If I had ignored those first two warnings, my third came a week later. After five straight nights of colic, and desperate for sleep, I raced to my parenting books for help. I quickly scanned the table of contents looking for "How to Cure Colic." The chapter I found was "Learning to Live with Colic." Things weren't working out exactly as I had planned.

Don't get me wrong. My beautiful baby girl was everything I'd ever dreamed she'd be and then some. David was a devoted father. Every time I saw his big arms wrapped so tenderly around our daughter, I felt myself fall deeper in love with him. It was me. I was disappointed in myself. I kept thinking, *What's wrong with me? I have the life*

I have dreamed of for ten years. Why am I not content here? Why am I not better at this? My sisters all have four and five children and make it look so easy.

In truth it was anything but easy. My friends back at the office were great, calling and coming by, sending gifts. *So why did I feel so totally and completely alone?* My husband did his best to help, but he knew nothing about babies and even less about the isolation I was feeling.

It was when I took out some pictures from my own childhood that I realized something. There was something in those pictures of my mother and me that was missing from my life with Haley—other moms and babies.

An acquaintance had mentioned a local nonprofit group called the "Parenting Center." I look back now and laugh when I think of how we must have looked that Monday morning, waiting in the parking lot of the building before the place even opened. Walking in the door, I felt shy. I was worried that they would look at me and know exactly how inadequate I was at this mommy thing. I felt like everyone there knew what she was doing but me. Then, a funny thing happened. I started to talk to some of the other moms. We talked about our deliveries, our recoveries, our sleepless nights, breast-feeding problems, even our mothers-in-law.

It was amazing. All of the self-doubt, all of the guilt, all of the feelings and experiences that to me had seemed mine alone, they, too, were feeling and experiencing. The things that had made me cry just the night before, I was now laughing about. We laughed about finally getting the baby to sleep and lying down ourselves, only to jump immediately up to check her breathing, about falling asleep in traffic, about putting a drop of baby shampoo in our own eye to make sure it was really tear-free. When I showed how I only got to manicure one hand before Haley began to cry and I had to stop, another mom rolled up her pants legs and showed how she had only shaved one leg. We laughed until we cried. I even told about calling 911 frantically because Haley was choking on water. I couldn't get enough of these women.

At times, we all talked at once. We even took to having a pad of paper and pen handy to jot down thoughts, so as not to forget what we wanted to say, when we got our chance to talk. I wasn't alone anymore. Here were people who were feeling the same things I was feeling and who had drastically changed their lives just as I had and for the same reasons. *With their support, I could do this. I could be the mom that Haley deserved.* As much as Haley depended on me for the things she needed, I began to depend on these women for reassurance, encouragement, and support.

It's been six years and two kids since my first visit to the "Parenting Center." Some of those women have come and gone from my life. But, some of them and their children have become part of our family.

No matter how crazy life gets during the week, I know that not far off there is a mom's-night-out when we can leave the kids at home and be kids ourselves. No matter how tight our finances may be, I know that I will soon be with my mom friends and will be reminded of why we are all doing this.

For me, staying home with my children was extremely important. I don't think I could have done it—I know I couldn't have done it as well—without the love and support of a dozen or so amazing women.

Mimi Greenwood Knight

Angel Hugs

What a child doesn't receive he can seldom later give.

P. D. James, *Time to Be in Earnest*

It's easy to lose hope when your child spends his or her first month in the hospital. It was a difficult pregnancy and our daughter was delivered via an emergency C-section seven weeks early. Her lungs weren't fully developed, and she had to be transported to a children's hospital nearly four hours away. Once there, our anticipated one- to two-week stay, through a series of setbacks and false starts, was extended to a full month of hospital visits and living in dirty hotel rooms.

You go numb after a while. You try to keep an even keel and try to take the setbacks in stride. I admit to feeling jealous when the other babies in the neonatal intensive care unit (NICU) were able to go home before our daughter, each time hoping that we'd be the next ones to leave. I felt helpless.

About three weeks into our stay, at the prodding of my parents, my wife and I decided to spend an afternoon together away from the hospital. My wife felt guilty for trying to enjoy herself while her daughter was in critical care, but we agreed that it was something that had to be done, for our sake.

We took a short trip to the city zoo. Being a veterinary technician, my wife is rather fond of animals and this seemed like a good way to unwind. Walking from one exhibit to another gave us ample time to share our feelings, clear our heads and hearts, and make lame (mostly on my part) attempts at humor. We encountered the humorous sight of a peacock, feathers on full display, engaged in a duel with its own reflection on the side of a metal trash can. We overheard a sad conversation between a young boy and his grandmother:

"Grandma, why do those men wear funny hats and dress alike?"

"That's because they're Amish. O-m-i-s-h." We didn't have the heart (or nerve) to correct her spelling, so we walked on.

The best thing that could have happened occurred soon after we walked in through the gates. Deciding to head off to see the gorillas and big cats first, we turned left onto the path, and in front of us stood a couple with their daughter. She was maybe five or six, obviously had Down's syndrome, and was absolutely beautiful with a radiant smile that could melt ice in a freezer from across the room. We returned her smile, touched by the look of utter happiness on her face. Then, without a word the little girl walked up to my wife and hugged her. The girl's parents immediately tried to apologize and pull her away, but I could sense that my wife was just as eager to keep on hugging her.

It's funny how signs like that can pop up here and there, letting you know that everything will be all right. Our daughter celebrated her first birthday this past week. In the words of my father, she's "spectacularly normal" for a one-year-old. She's very affectionate, and my hope is that one day she'll have a hug to give to someone who needs it, just like our little angel had one for us when we needed it most.

Kevin Butler

Organizing Tips

- Enlist your spouse to help keep easy and healthy snacks around and within arm's reach—it will be difficult to get meals in on a regular basis.

- You may have family members or friends that want to lend their support. Keep a list of chores handy for when others offer to help; for example, laundry, cooking, or running to the market.

- Keep an ongoing shopping list handy for when others offer to pick up something you may need at the market.

- Consider keeping one diaper bag with all the essentials in the car and a second one in the house with just basics ready to go each day (include water and fresh snacks for yourself).

- If you head out to lunch with a friend (and have your baby with you), it might be helpful to order your food to go or ask for a container "to go" ahead of time, just in case you need to head out ASAP if your baby is not up to hanging out.

Supportive Tips

- If your significant other can't stay overnight, consider asking a family member or hiring a baby nurse for extra support because hospitals can be low on staff. It makes a tremendous difference to have help getting out of bed to go to the bathroom or to have someone there to hand you the baby when he or she needs to be fed.

- Don't be shy. Enlist help from those who offer, but only if you feel they can provide the support you need.

- Respect the wide-ranging and diverse feelings that come up. They're more normal than you may think.

- Find a few trusted friends to share feelings with during this time.

- Talk to others about things that worked for them during pregnancy, labor, and the time period when they had a newborn—then make your own decision as to what you think will be best for yourself, your baby, and your family.

- Be gentle with yourself—the fatigue can catch up with you, and your hormones are all over the place.

- Avoid perfection! Allow some extra clutter for the first few months. Try to take it in stride. It's all about functionality during the newborn stage! For example, a second baby-changing area and a playpen in the living room may not look pretty, but it can make your day much easier.

- Don't be afraid to say no to visitors (except if they want to come over and help). This is the time when you need to focus more than ever on taking care of yourself, which will help you take care of your baby.

- Many women report feeling isolated at home with a newborn. Make an effort to get dressed each day (maybe even a bit of makeup) and get out of the house—even if it's just to take a walk around the block. Running into a neighbor for a brief chat may be a pleasant addition to your day.

- The saying comes up all the time—"It goes by so fast!" Embrace the here and now and make time to reflect on all the amazing moments of motherhood.

- Busy moms are always rushing to meet the needs and demands of their families. Making time to slow down and to stay present gives you the opportunity to capture moments that would otherwise slip away.

- If other family members aren't able to help out, consider hiring help at least one day per week in order to get time to nurture yourself.

- Incorporate humor into your life as much as possible. Laughter is an essential ingredient during our very busy days as moms.

4

A MOTHER'S LOVE

Love is the true means by which the world is enjoyed: our love to others and others' love to us.

Thomas Traherne

Birth of Understanding

Mother love is the fuel that enables a normal
human being to do the impossible.

Marion C. Garretty

I was once told that I couldn't understand because I didn't have children. A friend at work had been granted yet another personal day because her child was sick, and I felt it was unfair. I was offended by what she said, and somewhat resentful at being excluded from a club to which, at the time, I didn't even want to belong.

I thought about this the other night as I was rocking my son to sleep, trying to hide the tears streaming down my face at the thought of losing him.

I know now that my friend was not inflicting judgment on me. She was merely stating a truth. People who don't have kids simply can't understand what it's like to feel what parents feel. Now that I do understand, I'm still not sure sometimes that I want to belong to the club. Loving someone this much is frightening.

And in retrospect, it's something I've never truly done before.

It's not that I haven't always envisioned how it should be—pure, unconditional, eternal—because I have, and I've certainly had love in my life. Reality, though, is not always so kind. Relationships don't always work out, and after enough time and enough disappointment you learn, perhaps even unknowingly, to just give a part of yourself instead of the whole. That way when the ending inevitably comes, you've got something left.

Then you make this little human being and bring it into the world, and maybe for a few weeks you can keep your distance because after all, you're just getting to know each other. But slowly, slowly you start giving away pieces of your heart that you had forgotten existed, until one day you realize you couldn't survive if something happened to him. And you understand.

And it's not even just the thought of losing him. It's watching him change before your very eyes, knowing somehow that the acknowledgment of how fast he's growing won't slow down the time. Knowing that pictures from just yesterday can make you weep and long to go back. Knowing that the little sleepers he's already outgrown will forever represent an idyllic period of his life to which you can never return.

It's calling the doctor in the middle of the night because he has a fever, terrified of what you did wrong. It's the guilt of feeling responsible every time he gets a sniffle or an earache or cries when you don't know why. It's the sleepless nights holding him so tight because comforting him, sometimes, is all you can do. It's checking on him every five minutes to make sure he's breathing in his crib.

It's the need to protect him at all costs, and knowing that you simply can't. It's the overwhelming sadness that someday very soon he's going to walk out the door and you won't be there to save him from life's cruelties—the hurt and grief and pain from which you can't even protect yourself.

It's trying to memorize every pout, each gentle sigh, how he holds his tiny hands in front of his face in such complete awe, the bashful way he looks at you and smiles and burrows into your shoulder to sleep. It's knowing with a kind of bittersweet ache that these moments are as fleeting as snowflakes on his little cheek.

It's knowing that for the first time in your life you simply don't care about you, that nothing is more important than his health and happiness. It's knowing that you would give your own life, never to see or hold him again, if it could guarantee his own. It's knowing, finally, the meaning of true love, and fearing that it will be taken from you.

I once said that having my child was the hardest thing I would ever do, but I now understand that I was wrong.

Loving him is.

Maggie Lamond Simone

"I don't know about your mom, but mine
is spoiling me rotten."

Baby Shoes

I was in the children's shoe department when I experienced the revelation that would forever change how I looked at motherhood.

Here I was, a former professional "thirty-something" woman, standing in a daze for forty minutes in the children's shoe aisle of a department store, staring at baby shoes. I was extremely well researched in the correct methods of feeding, weaning, bonding, teething, burping, bathing, and time-outing! I had read those "What to Expect" books! It was difficult for me to accept that I was being tripped up, so to speak, by something as trivial as shoes!

As a new mother, I was too susceptible to the unsolicited opinions and popular current theories offered to me about the daily decisions I made for my child. While attempting to choose sneakers for my son, I noticed that the selection of shoes for his gender was adorned with superheroes, basketball stars, or brightly colored trains. Even though he was only two and a half, I couldn't bear for him to be "uncool" by choosing the trains, yet I also didn't want his feet to be a vehicle for advertising the latest Hollywood action film. I could have avoided this confusion had I gone to the popular athletic shoe stores at the mall, but it also didn't make sense for me to spend one hundred dollars on miniature replicas of what the NBA players would be wearing on the court this season, especially when he would outgrow them in a few months.

If I chose athletic gear for him to wear, was I pushing him to be too competitive? Was I pressuring him to adhere to masculine stereotypes? Not allowing him to "get in touch with his feminine side"? To counteract this possibility, I made sure that among the gifts Santa left on his first Christmas was a baby doll. He soon discovered that the doll worked equally well as a baseball bat. If I mentioned out loud that he loved to dance to music videos on TV, there always seemed to be some helpful mom present who felt compelled to tell me that her son wasn't allowed to watch music videos because of the "negative influences." If I allowed him to have a sip of soda as a treat on a hot day, I was looked at like I had offered him hemlock in a sippy cup!

The first time he bumped his head while trying to climb up on the sofa, he sustained an ugly purple bruise over his eyebrow. After having him checked out at the pediatrician's office, where they looked at me with that "You're wasting my time with *this*?" look, I took him out to his favorite fast-food place for some French fries, the kind fried in oil with very little nutritional value—bad, bad mommy! While in line, an older woman sidled up next to us and leaned over to whisper into my son's ear, "Did your mommy give you that boo-boo?" I realized that anyone who has had a child quickly becomes familiar with the little bumps and bruises that go along with learning how to walk and to climb, and that it is an unfortunate necessity in our society that well-meaning people are aware of the signs of abuse. Still, her comment stung, and later when my son fell on the gravel at the park and cut his lip,

I waited for it to heal completely before we ventured out in public again.

Strangers, who before I was a mother would have walked past me without a glance, now felt compelled to offer me all sorts of unsolicited advice. I suppose when I had my son, I had expectations of finally entering into the welcoming sisterhood of mothers. Sometimes it actually felt as though I had. A sympathetic smile when my son threw up on my leather jacket, a commiserating glance from the woman behind me in line at the grocery store while our collective two-year-olds demonstrated their tantrum skills. Other times, however, I felt as though everything I did for my child, from choosing his clothes and toys, to what I let him eat and watch on television, was open season for the "Mommy Police!"

At a time when we are most vulnerable, most in need of support, and most lacking in confidence, many new mothers are inundated with judgments and criticisms. They come in the form of well-meaning relatives and strangers, sound bites on the evening news, and competitive one-upmanship by other mothers on the playground. Before having my son, I had been a confident career woman. I had little difficulty making decisions, both professional and personal. I never dreamed that one day I would become so concerned about what strangers thought about the choices I made for my son that I could become momentarily paralyzed simply trying to decide which shoes to buy for him!

It was at that moment, however, that the answer finally dawned on me. I took a good look at my son sitting happy, healthy, bright, and beaming on the floor in front of me. He was lovingly holding a pair of Batman sneakers. He was fine. He was safe. He was secure. Most important, he was mine. I realized that maybe it wasn't all the choices that confounded me, or even all the opinions constantly thrown at me that shook my confidence in being a good mother. It was that in all my life before him, no decision I had ever made had been as important to me as him. It didn't matter if he had action heroes on his sneakers or that he preferred bright, colorful, plastic toys to sturdy, wooden, environmentally conscious ones. It wasn't important if the cartoons that he loved were entertaining as opposed to educational, or that he preferred rap to Beethoven. All that mattered was that he was safe and happy.

We left the store, hand in hand, my son lifting his Batman feet high, every inch a superhero! We got French fries and soda at our local fast-food restaurant that had an indoor playground. I sipped my coffee (regular with caffeine), while I watched him having a wonderful time playing in the ball pit. I've been told that in some places, the balls aren't cleaned regularly and could be considered unsanitary.

They looked fine to me.

Lisa Duffy-Korpics

Wishes

I wished for some rest, some quiet, some time to pursue the interests expressed pre-children. I even imagined a housekeeper from breakfast to dinner to fix meals and take care of my two children, and even though pregnant, I fantasized closing myself in a room to paint, model with clay, sew dresses, and so on, knowing all outside that door was in order.

Running a house and raising children without help is a full-time, fatigue-filled task. The feeling of accomplishment is short lived: a freshly waxed kitchen floor after breakfast becomes a playground for muddy feet, spilled milk, oozed jelly from a sandwich; a vacuumed rug gets the cracker sprays; polished furniture lends itself well to fresh finger marks; washed woodwork is tempting to dirty fingers or bright crayons.

In college, I minored in art. I could spend a month on a canvas preparing colors, applying them, being satisfied or disappointed, but when the painting was completed, the feeling of accomplishment was there. So did playing a musical instrument fulfill after much tedious practice. I taught secondary school, before the birth of my own children, and could actually see achievements measured by standard exams or watch the face of a pupil as a new concept was grasped. Now I saw shiny silver tarnishing, crisply ironed dresses wrinkle in a few minutes, "creative" meals ingested at a rapid pace, shiny shoes scuffed, and a clean bathroom sink at eleven o'clock holding worms by noon.

Our fifth move in seven years seemed more difficult as I was six months pregnant plus had a four-and-a-half-year-old son and a two-and-half-year-old daughter. Packing and unpacking and resettling were chaotic. This only increased my yearnings for time for me . . . dust off brushes that hadn't been used for nearly a decade, play the piano that remained closed most often, time to think. I so wanted to rest and have someone wait on me. Like all mothers, no matter how ill I've ever felt, I could not go to bed. I've no office to phone and say I need to stay home today, and children must eat no matter how ill a mother feels. I also knew that my short hospital stay would be anything but a relaxed rest.

How I wished for someone to come in and "take over" while I'd return late in the day and just enjoy my children already bathed, dinner someone else had prepared, a house nicely straightened.

Within weeks, I developed thrombophlebitis, a disorder affecting the veins in the legs, and was immediately sent to bed with only bathroom privileges. Some person came in and "took over." My meals were brought to me. My children played on my bed, and we enjoyed one another's company without my having to do chores for them. Of course I couldn't paint or play the piano, but a friend brought me all the books I'd longed to read. This wasn't quite the way I'd wished, however. The first few days of reading were marvelous, but the household was not shut out merely because I was confined to the bedroom. The seriousness of a clot was a high price to pay for a gift of a partially fulfilled wish.

Once I was up and in charge of my own home and kitchen, I realized how wonderful that was. Someone else can adore my children and care for them, but only I can give them a heritage. Anyone may read to them, but I can draw from my storehouse of precious education and try to expose them to all there is to learn. Another can cook my meals, but no one else may make my husband able to brag about his wife's cakes or my children to recall (as adults) how their mother used to prepare specific dishes.

Running a house and raising children is still a fatigue-filled, full-time occupation, yet striving to accomplish the goal of preparing children to be healthy, intelligent, com-passionate, unselfish human beings is greater in labor and reward than realized. Healthy offspring and worms in the bathroom basin are better than a clean, quiet, home where illness prevails. In my own way, I create daily, no longer as a co-ed or school teacher, without a status title. I under-stood, for real, that bearing a child is a privilege; being entrusted with its life, an honor; guiding to grow into adulthood, an enormous responsibility; permitting the young freedom to develop, a gift. Lucky me.

Lois Greene Stone

Mother Knows Best

God could not be everywhere, so he created mothers.

Jewish Proverb

After the birth of my twin daughters, my mother offered to stay for a week and help out. Being a naive new mom I figured I didn't really need her help. *How hard could it be?* I thought I was the youthful, energetic one, newly imbued through the labor and delivery of two babies, with an innate knowledge of how to care for them. My mom was nearing sixty, and although she had raised three children, well, that was a long time ago. I agreed to her offer, glad for the company, but not from a perception of need.

My mother came, saw what needed to be done, and very quietly did it. Always with a smile, she made meals, including the entire Thanksgiving dinner for six that I thought I could handle on my own. She cleaned, shopped, did laundry, and rocked screaming babies in the small hours of the morning. She never once did the thing I most feared she would do: lecture me on the myriad things I could do better or differently. She never once gave unsolicited advice. She did, however, frequently tell me what every new mom desperately needs to hear—that I was doing a great job.

I was endlessly amazed by her energy, her competency, and her unflappable, easy manner with my daughters. I stumbled around in a fog of bleary-eyed exhaustion, going through the motions of motherhood, while she busily snapped pictures and exclaimed over the marvels of my babies.

She was always one step ahead of me, even though I swear she got less sleep. I wondered if this was the same mother I remembered from my high school years, back when I knew everything, and she knew less than everything; back when I rolled my eyes at her a lot and she spent a lot of time trying to tell me that there were things I wouldn't understand until I became a mother myself.

The last vestiges of my myopic, know-it-all adolescence died the week after my daughters were born. And good riddance. Because in its place a new understanding was born—an understanding with a lot more respect and much better vision.

I had known I would become a new mom when I had children, but I never realized that I would also get a new mom—my same wonderful old mom, the one I never truly saw.

Karen Crafts Driscoll

My Daughter's Hands

My daughter Miriam had a cold and was having trouble sleeping, so tonight I had the distinct pleasure of rocking her—for a long, long time—to sleep. We sat there in her dark room, the rocking chair creaking slightly, her slow, even breaths a little raspy from her cold. Her head was nuzzled into my neck, and her right hand softly gripped the fabric of my shirt on my chest.

Miriam's hand. It's a plump little thing, dimpled, smooth, and creamy white. I've always been fascinated by my children's hands, but tonight as I looked at Miriam's, I was overwhelmed with happiness, and a little sadness, to think of where those hands will travel. Tonight they're flawless little hands, untested by life's challenges and inexperienced in its joys. But where will those little hands go tomorrow, and the next day and the next?

One day soon those little hands will let go of mine as she takes her first step.

They'll grasp a pencil as she clumsily but surely learns to write.

They'll grip bicycle handlebars with a mix of joy and horror as her daddy runs behind her holding on, almost ready to let go.

In her teenage years those hands will wipe away many adolescent tears and slam many doors, but maybe, if I play my cards right, they'll still reach out for mine every now and then.

They'll pack her belongings as she leaves home. And they'll open our front door again as she comes back to visit. Often, if she knows what's good for her.

How I pray those precious hands spend more time spread open in joy, rather than clenched in anguish. But wherever they travel, I hope they're often clasped in prayer. I hope they're helpful hands, and merciful ones, and I hope they always have many, many other hands to grab onto.

They'll wear a diamond from a handsome young man, and they'll loosely hold her father's tuxedoed arm, eager to reach out for her future at the end of the aisle.

Those hands will grasp the bedsheets in pain as she fights to deliver her child, and they'll tremble in joy when she holds him or her for the first time. They'll feel many little foreheads, apply many Band-Aids, and hold open many books. And then, one night, she'll rock that baby to sleep, and she'll stare in bittersweet wonder at its little hands.

Shannon Lowe

READER/CUSTOMER CARE SURVEY

We care about your opinions! Please take a moment to fill out our online Reader Survey at **http://survey.hcibooks.com**. As a **"THANK YOU"** you will receive a **VALUABLE INSTANT COUPON** towards future book purchases as well as a **SPECIAL GIFT** available only online! Or, you may mail this card back to us and we will send you a copy of our exciting catalog with your valuable coupon inside.

First Name _____ MI. _____ Last Name _____

Address _____

State _____ Zip _____ Email _____ City _____

1. Gender
- ❑ Female ❑ Male

2. Age
- ❑ 8 or younger
- ❑ 9-12 ❑ 13-16
- ❑ 17-20 ❑ 21-30
- ❑ 31+

3. Did you receive this book as a gift?
- ❑ Yes ❑ No

4. Annual Household Income
- ❑ under $25,000
- ❑ $25,000 - $34,999
- ❑ $35,000 - $49,999
- ❑ $50,000 - $74,999
- ❑ over $75,000

5. What are the ages of the children living in your house?
- ❑ 0 - 14 ❑ 15+

6. Marital Status
- ❑ Single ❑ Married
- ❑ Divorced ❑ Widowed

7. How did you find out about the book?
(please choose one)
- ❑ Recommendation
- ❑ Store Display
- ❑ Online
- ❑ Catalog/Mailing
- ❑ Interview/Review

8. Where do you usually buy books?
(please choose one)
- ❑ Bookstore
- ❑ Online
- ❑ Book Club/Mail Order
- ❑ Price Club (Sam's Club, Costco's, etc.)
- ❑ Retail Store (Target, Wal-Mart, etc.)

9. What subject do you enjoy reading about the most?
(please choose one)
- ❑ Parenting/Family
- ❑ Relationships
- ❑ Recovery/Addictions
- ❑ Health/Nutrition
- ❑ Christianity
- ❑ Spirituality/Inspiration
- ❑ Business Self-help
- ❑ Women's Issues
- ❑ Sports

10. What attracts you most to a book?
(please choose one)
- ❑ Title
- ❑ Cover Design
- ❑ Author
- ❑ Content

TAPE IN MIDDLE; DO NOT STAPLE

BUSINESS REPLY MAIL

FIRST-CLASS MAIL PERMIT NO 45 DEERFIELD BEACH, FL

POSTAGE WILL BE PAID BY ADDRESSEE

Chicken Soup for the New Mom's Soul
3201 SW 15th Street
Deerfield Beach, FL 33442-9875

FOLD HERE

Do you have your own Chicken Soup story
that you would like to send us?
Please submit at: **www.chickensoup.com**

Comments

Promises

Before you were conceived I wanted you.
Before you were born I loved you.
Before you were here an hour I would die for
you.
This is the miracle of love.

Maureen Hawkins

My hands trembled as I took the tiny infant in my arms. After a long labor and a difficult pregnancy, I was ecstatic to hold my newborn son. He was especially precious, as my first pregnancy had ended in a miscarriage at four months. Weighing in at barely six pounds, he seemed so tiny and delicate.

"Mrs. Rodman, you can have him with you as long as you like," the nurse said. "Your husband left to go buy cigars," she added with a chuckle under her breath.

"Are you sure it's okay? He's so small, he looks like he'll break," I replied with fear in my voice.

"Oh, they all look like that, you're not used to a newborn yet. Just remember to keep your arm under his head," she instructed, and with that she was gone.

Barely twenty years old, I was so scared and naive. I had never before held such a tiny infant. I knew nothing of babies, of child rearing, of discipline, or of parenting in general. I was going to have to buy lots of child care books.

I had tried on some of our possible names: *Joseph? Michael? Patrick? Ah, now there was a strong Irish name, Patrick.* I said it out loud a couple times, "Patrick, Patrick." I liked the ring of it. Patrick it would be, with the middle name Francis. Patrick Francis Rodman.

My husband would agree with my choice. Besides, Francis was my husband's father's name, my sister's middle name, my father's middle name, and my grand-mother's maiden name. We could make a lot of people happy with that one!

Patrick's sky-blue eyes stared up at me in wonder; at least I like to think they did. As I twirled his patch of little blond peach-fuzz hair around my finger, I fell hopelessly head over heels in love.

I decided to get this "motherhood thing" off to a good start with our first heart-to-heart chat, never mind that it was well past 2:00 AM. Talking always calmed my fears, and I was afraid. This was going to be a big responsibility, rais-ing a son, and I hoped I could do it right.

"I promise to be the best mom I know how, but you're going to have to be patient with me. I've never done this before," I explained.

He gurgled and cooed, which I was sure meant that he agreed. I told him of the dreams I had for him, the nursery that awaited his homecoming, the things we would do together, and the ways he could make me proud to be his mother.

"I want you to be a caring person with a good heart. I want you to have good values. I want you to love life and live each day to the fullest. I want you to value education and make your way in the world. But most of all, Patrick, I want you to promise you'll always keep in touch, no matter how far away from home the world takes you." I went on to explain other things I thought he should know.

We ended our first talk just as dawn broke over the lawn outside.

"Patrick, you better go to the nursery now and get some rest. You've had a big day and so have I." And with that I rang for the nurse.

As time went by, I learned parenting wasn't as hard as it looked, although it had its trying moments. I went on to have two more children, but Patrick was my only son. Patrick and I remained close through the ups and downs of childhood. He had his share of snits and fits as a teenager, but we managed to continue our heart-to-heart chats through the years.

It wasn't long before he was off to college. He called me often from the dorms. He went on to a successful career and recently married, but at least once a week the phone will ring.

"What's new, Mom?" Patrick will say. "Just called to check in."

I think of our very first chat so long ago and I smile, remembering a scared young mother and a tiny baby boy with sky-blue eyes. He has kept his promises and I have kept mine.

Sallie A. Rodman

In the Beginning

The only thing worth stealing is a kiss from a sleeping child.

Joe Houldsworth

I should have known what motherhood would be like, considering the way it started. By dawn's early light, I followed Mac out to our VW bug, ready to bring our first child into the world. He started the engine, shifted into reverse, and we backed down the driveway.

"What's that smell?" I sniffed the air. "Smells like somebody stepped in something." Mac stopped the car, and we both got out to check our shoes. Sure enough, my left sneaker was coated with the reminder of what the neighborhood dogs felt right at home leaving in our front yard. Giggling between labor pains, I wiped my shoe on the grass and our journey resumed.

At the hospital, I was prepped and settled into the labor room. Twelve hours and several roommates later, I produced a round, red, squalling object. My firstborn. My son. Five days later we took our bundle of joy home, and I began my career as a mom.

Like most first-timers, I had no idea what I was getting into. I'd done some babysitting, of course, but this night-and-day routine was bigger than life. Especially the nights. The first night home, both Mac and I hovered over the lacy white bassinet, straining to hear breathing sounds. By the second night, Mac was snoozing through hungry cries, and I was dragging myself from the comfort of our double bed to tend the most demanding individual I'd ever encountered.

Did he really have to eat every three hours? Could he really need a clean diaper that often? In the days before disposables, those didies had to be washed, dried, and folded to fit little bottoms—an all-day chore in itself. And the rest of his laundry! Every diaper change included a fresh gown, a dry T-shirt, and often, clean socks. Receiving blankets and tiny sheets filled the washer. Even when the diapers stayed dry, the clothes of both baby and parents had to be laundered. I could swear that child spit back more milk than he took in.

Mac returned to work after a few days, and I settled into a routine of sleep-deprived drudgery. Not that I didn't love the little nipper. Those daylight moments when young Mitch was full, dry, and content were heavenly. But, oh, those nights! As Mac walked the floor with an armful of screaming baby, he told me something he'd learned in the army—that a seven-pound weight, such as a rifle or an infant, seems to double every fifteen minutes when it's carried. Didn't I know it!

We rocked, walked, jiggled, and juggled—anything for a minute of peace. We fed and overfed, changed and checked for open pins. There just had to be a reason our baby was so unhappy. We desperately needed to find and fix the problem. Dad became practiced at sighing. Mom often dissolved into tears. I was sure my baby had a serious medical problem, no matter what his doctor said.

Then it happened. A four-hour stretch without a peep. It was dark and baby was sleeping. *Was he still breathing?* I touched the tiny body. It was warm and squirmed beneath my fingers. *Whatever you do, don't wake him up!* I tiptoed back to bed and waited for his wake-up call. After four hours of uninterrupted sleep, I felt I could conquer the world.

Of course, I was never called upon to conquer the world. My job was simply to raise my son and his younger sister to adulthood. Know what? I did it. Mac and I did it without training or instruction of any kind. Did we do everything perfect or even right? No, but our kids are still speaking to us, and I take that as a good sign.

One lasting effect of those early years—they taught me the value of a good night's sleep.

June Williams

The Naked Truth

When our daughter Micah was two weeks old, I decided to have her portrait taken at a local studio. Flipping through the photographer's portfolio, I saw darling black-and-white shots of sleepy, naked, newborn babies.

"That's what I want," I said, pointing to a bald baby resting facedown with her knees tucked underneath her stomach and her bottom in the air.

Another pose showed a nude infant stretching in his daddy's hands. The pictures were simply precious! Micah was barely five pounds, and I wanted the naked photos to emphasize her skinny legs and tiny arms. I made an appointment for later that week.

"Are you sure you want to do this?" asked my husband, Michael. "Two weeks old seems a little soon for a photo shoot."

I rolled my eyes. "Nonsense! Anne Geddes does it all the time. Those sleepy newborn baby shots have made her famous."

"I don't know," answered Michael. "It sounds like a bad idea."

I walked out of the room. *Photographing a sleeping baby— how hard could that be?*

Later that week, we buckled the baby into her infant carrier and attached it to the base in the backseat. It was only the second time that Micah had been in the car since she came home from the hospital. As we drove to the 7:00 PM appointment, she cried and yelled.

"What do you think is wrong with her?" Michael asked.

For the last few days, I noticed Micah seemed fussier in the late afternoon and evening hours. She had developed symptoms of colic, crying inconsolably. What was I thinking, making a nighttime appointment?

"You know every time we take her clothes off, she screams," my husband reminded me as we pulled into the parking lot.

My stomach somersaulted. Maybe Michael was right. This might not be such a good idea.

Inside the studio, I gently removed my baby's onesie. Micah wasn't sleepy like those other babies whose photographs adorned the walls. She didn't wear a sweet, serene look on her face, either. After a few minutes her scowl gave way to wails. Anne Geddes would have been sorely disappointed.

"Maybe she's hungry," suggested the photographer, who boasted that her four-month-old daughter always fell asleep after nursing. "Take your time and feed her. I'll come back in a few minutes."

The baby nursed a little, but mostly she just flailed her arms, screaming and crying.

Michael looked on sympathetically. "Honey, I know you want these pictures, but . . ."

"It will be fine," I interrupted, but deep down I wished we'd stayed home.

Micah wanted no part of the naked photo shoot, even after feeding.

"Try swaddling her," said the photographer. I wrapped Micah in her receiving blanket, but that didn't seem to help much either. Moments after removing the cover, I was posing Micah in front of the camera. I had one hand on her back and the other under her bare bottom. All of a sudden, she quit crying. Her face changed. *She must like that position,* I thought. Then, ever so gently, a little glob of poop dropped into my palm.

Michael grabbed a baby wipe from the diaper bag as I apologized profusely to the photographer.

"I think we should go now," he whispered, as he cleaned up the mess.

The photographer assured me she'd taken enough shots to ensure a good variety, but I doubted she'd gotten even one.

Two weeks later, I picked up the proofs and although there were no sleeping baby poses, there were quite a few cute pictures. It was another three weeks before our prints arrived.

I procrastinated on getting them framed right away. There was always so much to do with a new baby, and quite honestly, the ordeal at the photographer's was still fresh in my memory. Finally, I took the pictures to the framing shop. The clerk unwrapped the package and laid on the counter seven different poses in four-by-six, five-by-seven, and eight-by-ten prints. One shot showed Micah's head cradled in my hands, her body so small on my forearms that her feet didn't reach my elbow. A close-up featured her fingers wrapped around her daddy's thumb. One portrait showed Micah sitting in the palm of my hand, her delicate legs crossed at the ankles.

I stood amazed, my gaze transfixed on the tiny infant in the picture. *Was she really that small?*

It had only been a few weeks ago that we drove across town with a colicky baby for newborn photographs. I almost couldn't believe that was the same child. Micah was now three months old, more than double her birth weight and five inches longer than the infant in those black-and-white portraits. I'd forgotten how frail she was and how the skin on her arms and legs hung in wrinkles.

"Something wrong, ma'am?" asked the clerk.

"Oh, no," I replied, as tears welled up in the corners of my eyes. "It's just that she's grown so much since we took these. I forgot."

Now, instead of reliving the trauma of that first photo shoot, I felt only gratitude that I'd captured her image on film. Seeing Micah's first pictures was an awakening to the realization that she was developing more than I noticed on a daily basis. Days turn to weeks, time creeps by, and before I knew it my baby would be grown. Instead of the serene, sleeping baby portrait I coveted, I got an important lesson in parenting. I must learn to relish each day with my growing daughter. Those photos remind me that time is short and passes all too quickly for mothers.

Stephanie Welcher Thompson

Organizing Tips

- Schedule time in your busy days and meet up with other moms. This also creates an informal support system.

- Schedule self-nurturing appointments for yourself to make sure you get them in.

- Consider purchasing a special journal to capture your feelings about your motherhood experience down on paper.

Supportive Tips

- Our love for our children is so profound and deep—we can feel so vulnerable. Know that you're not alone!

- We give so much because the love for our children is tremendous; it's truly beyond what words can adequately describe, but we must take some time-out to nurture ourselves. Even the most patient moms need to replenish their energy.

5

DADDY DEAR

I could not point to any need in childhood as strong as that for a father's protection.

Sigmund Freud

If You Need Help—Ask!

Nothing had prepared me for the moment my son was born. Not the books I was told to read about parenting. Not the educational degrees I had earned in college. Not even the twenty-plus years I had spent as a teacher and coach. When that delivery room nurse walked in and handed him to me for the first time, I suddenly realized what my wife had been trying to tell me for quite some time: I WAS CLUELESS!

I felt like a lineman holding a football trying not to fumble it. The nurse must have sensed my apprehension, so she stuck around just in case. When my son started to get fussy, I looked at her with fear in my eyes and said, "What do I do?"

She looked at me with a smile on her face and said, "What do you know how to do?"

"Nothing!" was my frantic reply.

The words she spoke next were pretty profound. "Remember, Dad, when you need help, ask."

The next three days began my crash course on fatherhood. Everything from feeding to burping to changing dirty diapers was thrust upon me. Where I once viewed myself as a competent teacher and coach, I now found myself totally incompetent. My wife found humor in my awkwardness, but to me it was hard to take. The simplest tasks seemed difficult. I used to coach athletic teams with a steady hand. Work through student's problems with calmness. Now, suddenly, I found myself panicky when left alone with my infant son. All the while he looked at me like I was the greatest thing on earth. Boy, if he only knew!

Using the advice the nurse gave me I asked a lot of questions. Day by day, things became easier. I sought advice from local experts who had already gone through the "basic training" of parenthood. I became amazed at how little a pediatrician knew compared with a veteran mommy. I learned to listen and actually read directions. Never before considering myself to be particularly handy with tools, it was amazing how quickly I learned to put together a baby bed, fix a stroller, and assemble a newly purchased toy.

Through all this I found a new confidence. Strange, but no matter how many games you win as a coach, it doesn't compare with quieting a fussy baby as a way to boost a man's morale.

When discussing what I had watched on Disney TV became a bigger part of my conversations than the highlights from ESPN SportsCenter, I knew the transformation to fatherhood was well under way. Becoming a father taught me a lesson in humility. It is a lesson I pass on to others. Forget about pride. When you need help, ask.

Tom Krause

Love Has No Borders

Rocking my two-year-old before her nap, I was not surprised when Savannah wanted to talk instead of closing her eyes to sleep.

Always fighting sleep to the bitter end, Savannah often points to various objects and questions, "Who gots it for me?" That day, she pointed to the teddy-bear border in her room. I smiled and replied, "Your daddy put up your teddy-bear paper. You are so lucky to have such a good daddy!"

Looking at the border with its mismatched teddy bears in one corner and the buckling piece of paper not sealed with glue in the other corner, I seriously doubt that it would meet the approval of an interior decorator. However, I truly believe that even Martha Stewart would approve of the love behind the hanging of this border.

After struggling with infertility, hormone treatments, and a heartbreaking miscarriage, news of being pregnant with Savannah brought me great joy, as well as many worries. Knowing that I could lose another precious child, I just could not relax during my second pregnancy. Due to my fears, the nursery was still not decorated when I was seven months pregnant. Then, when my awkward seven-months-pregnant body fell and I twisted my ankle, my fear that I harmed the baby was overwhelming.

` My husband, Terry, decided to stay home from work. His decision resulted in more than his "babying" me. It was when I also realized how lucky I was to not only have this wonderful man as my husband, but also what a special daddy he was going to be.

One day, after a much needed nap, I found Terry in the baby's room. "Surprise! How do you like the border?" Terry asked. Hanging the teddy-bear border was Terry's special way of reassuring me that our baby was going to be just fine.

This was only the beginning of how Terry would show that his love for his family truly has no boundaries. Not only does he continue to support me in dealing with various parenting fears (presently, cooling high temperatures and controlling a two-year-old's temper tantrums), but he also shows his love by folding clothes, picking up toys, and changing dirty diapers without being asked. His love and support not only help our time together as a family be more relaxing and enjoyable, but also results in my being a better mother.

Whether it is helping with household chores, reading Savannah's favorite book countless times, or sitting in Savannah's Big Bird chair waiting for her tea party, Terry's acts of love truly show that a daddy's love has no boundaries when it comes to his family's happiness.

As I glance at the wallpaper one more time, I whisper to a now sleeping Savannah, "Yes, Savannah. You're so lucky to have such a good daddy. God truly has blessed you, as well as your mom. I am so lucky to have you and also a husband whose love for his family has no borders."

Stephanie Ray Brown

A Constant Presence

Our son, Mason, came into this world the usual way. Dave and I married late in life and were very eager to start our family. When we did get pregnant, we shared every moment of those nine months, from doctor visits to readying the nursery to baby showers and even gaining weight! Mason finally arrived in October 2003, just in time for his daddy to be deployed to Iraq.

A longtime member of the California Army National Guard, Dave had received his orders just days before Mason came into this world. He left us for an eighteen-month tour in the Middle East when Mason was only three weeks old.

As a new first-time mom—a new, *single* first-time mom—I found myself with a baby boy. A boy, I cried to myself. Boys need their dads to help mold them into men. Through many tears, some from fear of my husband fighting in a war zone and many from postpartum blues, I made the decision to mother Mason with strength, joy, and, most important, Dave's presence. I set my goal to provide a safe and loving environment for our son and to bridge the gap between our home in northern California and the hot, sandy deserts of Iraq.

I was determined to make sure Mason not only knew his father when he finally came home, but that our son would be excited to see him. I purchased six-inch wooden letters that read "My Daddy," as well as several picture frames, filling them with large photos of Dave, both in uniform and in civilian clothes. Then I arranged them all on the wall overlooking Mason's crib, screwing everything into place so he couldn't pull them down on himself.

Next, I laminated pictures of Dave and gave them to Mason to play with, put in his mouth, carry around the house, give to the family dog, or whatever he wanted to do with them. The goal was for Mason to learn his father's face, his daddy's eyes and smile.

One day, when Mason was just seven months old, we were at our favorite local restaurant when a soldier entered wearing the traditional camouflage. Mason stared at him, obviously recognizing the uniform. My plan was working!

Meanwhile, greeting cards began arriving in the mail from Dave. Before he was deployed, he must have secretly purchased lots of beautiful and funny cards to send as a surprise, along with wonderful letters. This amazing gesture of love by Dave equated to some of my most favorite mother-and-son bonding times. The two of us snuggled in the special rocker in Mason's room, with me reading the letters out loud while he gummed the cards, making a slobbery mess. And even though I sometimes read Dave's letters through my tears, I felt strongly that Mason understood that the letters and cards were from his daddy. I knew he realized that there was more to "us" than just him and me.

As Mason grew and his development progressed, I put the telephone to his ear when Dave called home. His eyes would light up; he squirmed all over my lap with excitement. At eleven months, Mason started bringing me his play telephone, holding out the receiver, and saying, "Da-Da, Da-Da."

Time passed quickly, and finally my son and I headed to the base to pick up Dave. The question kept running through my brain: Was I successful in keeping Dave's presence a constant in Mason's heart and in our home? Would his baby boy know him? I fretted that since Mason had experienced very little physical contact with his daddy after his first three weeks of life, he would not know his father.

Then Dave stepped off the bus and raced toward us. Mason immediately reached for him, took his daddy's face in his little hands, and exclaimed with a big smile, "Da-Da!"

Kathleen Partak

My Father's Tears

My dad was always the strong silent type. Growing up, I rarely saw him angry, or even raise his voice in debate. He was often miserable with allergies, but didn't take it out on us. He never told me he loved me—that was just not his way. This was difficult for me when I was young.

I remember one time I cried and cried. Finally my mother reached out and comforted me. Then my father said the words I so wanted to hear. When you have to put up a fuss to hear someone say "I love you," it makes the words feel empty and of little consolation. Yet deep inside I knew he loved me. Through all these growing-up years, I never saw him cry.

Years later, my first son—his first grandson—was born. He was born in the dark, cold, early-morning hours of a winter blizzard. Still exhausted and scared, I called my parents. With the storm raging, they could only "try to make it" the next day.

My husband and I were both students and very poor. We had no means to pay the hospital, so I had a very limited stay. Exhausted and numb from the emotional waves of ecstasy and despair, I wanted to stay longer. Late in the afternoon of the next day, my hospital roommate left for a walk and snack. I had my sleeping baby with me. I tried to sleep, but could not.

I was startled at the sound of light knocking. The nurse peeked in. "I know it isn't visiting hours," she said, "but this is a special visitor."

There, standing in the doorway, was my dad, terribly out of place. He was still in his dirty old work coat. The dirt on his hands and face told me he came straight from work. He had a blue carnation in a small white vase tied with a blue ribbon. I guessed he picked it up at the hospital gift shop.

He looked at me sheepishly as he crept a little way into the room. My eyes met his. I saw a tear in his eye. It welled up and gently rolled down his cheek. And then another. And another. I never saw my father cry before—the silent emotion was overwhelming.

"See your grandson?" I blurted out trying to hide my own feeling of awkwardness. But it was useless. Tears glazed over my eyes as well.

We were both in tears as he gingerly made his way closer and handed me the carnation. He slowly stretched to peek at the baby, keeping his distance. He stayed only briefly and then he was gone.

Although few words were spoken that visit, it touched me deeply. I knew beyond any doubt that my father loved me and was proud of me. Those tears will forever be in my heart.

Robin Clifton

Birth of a Father

Horror. Sheer horror. That's what I felt when I saw a videotape of a baby's birth during childbirth classes. Don't get me wrong. I always wanted kids. But somehow, I never really thought about the process of *having* them. Seeing a birth video, so up close and personal, quite frankly terrified me.

As the childbirth instructor turned on the lights, I leaned over to comment on the absurdity of that woman being shown in such an unflattering situation. My wife, Stephanie, who *used* to be my cohort in seeing the comedy in situations, now dabbed her eyes with a tissue.

"Isn't it wonderful?" she gushed.

Hormones had turned my predictable, stable wife into this weepy woman.

After seeing that tape, I was adamant about not viewing the birth of our baby. I conceded to coach breathing exercises during labor, but when it came time for the actual delivery, I envisioned myself seated in a chair at the head of the bed holding my wife's hand.

"Delivery is the touchdown," joked our birthing coach. "You wouldn't sit through four quarters of the Super Bowl then go to the fridge if the score was tied, your team had the ball on the two-yard line, and there was less than a minute left in the game, would you?"

In the back of my mind, I knew there was no way I could stomach seeing our baby being born, or for that matter, change a diaper. So, I made a game plan. My idea was to put in extra hours before the birth.

I became Stephanie's "go-to guy." For some reason, pregnancy made her too tired to do anything but work and sleep, so I grocery shopped, ran errands, cooked meals, and did the household chores.

Week by week, I read excerpts about how both mother and fetus were changing.

"Your body is growing precious cargo," I'd reassure her when she was emotional (again). "It's taking all your energy to make our baby."

When her back hurt, I rubbed. When her feet ached, I massaged. I knew my slave labor would pay off in the end. I did more than my share around the house, but there was one thing I refused to compromise on. I repeatedly told Stephanie that I wanted to sit in the stands rather than be on the field during the actual birth. Translation: I'm here for you, honey, but don't expect me to do much more than coach your breathing.

"In fact, I don't want to look at the baby until she's properly cleaned," I emphasized. "And, changing a diaper is out of the question. I'll vomit."

I knew I'd love our child, but the day-to-day care was Stephanie's job. I was very clear about that. When our child was old enough to take to the football stadium, then I'd lend a hand. But, care for an infant? Not my game.

Every preconceived notion I had about fatherhood changed once our daughter was born.

I went without meals for twenty-three hours when Stephanie was in labor. "Hee, hee, hee, haa. . . ." I coached her breathing and held her arm as she walked the halls.

When nurses called the doctor to "catch" the baby, I walked over to the dry erase board in the hospital room and wrote: "Happy Birthday, Micah." Relieved that my job was done, I took a seat near the head of the bed and prepared to watch the labor and delivery team do their magic.

A few minutes later, one of the nurses shouted, "Dad, we need your help with pushing."

Didn't she get the memo? I held on tight to Stephanie's hand and anchored myself firmly in the chair. "I'm fine right here," I replied, with a weak smile.

"Now, Dad," she yelled, grabbing my arm.

I was thrust into the middle of the action. She positioned me at the bottom of the bed and shoved Stephanie's foot into my stomach. Then, she grabbed my hands and wrapped them around my wife's shin.

"There, now," she said enthusiastically. "This will give you a perfect view of the birth."

I felt the color drain from my face.

Breathe, I told myself. If I fainted, Stephanie would never let me live it down.

A few minutes later, the baby crowned.

"I see black hair," I shouted. All of the sudden, my dread turned to excitement.

Our daughter Micah was born and the doctor immediately handed the baby (not properly cleaned) to me— even before Stephanie got to hold her. I felt an overwhelming wave of emotion for this blanketed bundle. How was it possible to have such a strong feeling of love so quickly? My baby's grayish eyes blinked through the messy white cream that covered her face. She was the most beautiful thing I'd ever seen.

The nurse wanted to put Micah under warming lights.

"Honey, I don't want to leave you, but I think I should go with the baby to make sure she's all right," I told Stephanie.

"Hey, there, little girl," I cooed, as I stroked her tiny hand. "It's okay. Daddy's here."

Moments later, our families came in and I proudly displayed our newborn. "Here's your grandpa, little girl," I heard myself say in a lilting voice.

During the rest of our hospital stay, our baby was never out of my sight. Around midnight, a nurse slipped in to take Micah down the hall to run some tests. She said she'd be back in about an hour.

"I'll come with you," I called, from the foldout couch.

"That's okay, Dad," she replied. "You get some rest."

My baby wasn't going anywhere without me. I pulled on my shoes. "Wait." The stern tone in my voice surprised me.

The commotion awakened Stephanie.

"I'll change her diaper before you go," she said, sitting up from the bed.

"No, honey, you rest," I replied. "I need to practice changing her."

Steph tried to look nonchalant as I gently lifted Micah's legs and fumbled to get the diaper around her six-pound body, but I knew what she was thinking: twelve hours old and already she's got you wrapped around her matchstick-sized pinkie.

It was true. She was Daddy's girl.

Micah is now three years old and the pride of my heart. She's baptized me in bodily fluids and blessed me with giggles. I've shared in the good (when "da da" was her first word), the bad (when as a newborn she had jaundice and had to be strapped to a light table for seventy-two hours), and the ugly (when six-month-old Micah caught a virus and spit vomit in my face) aspects of parenthood.

There's a big discrepancy between the way I planned to be a father and the dad I've become. But, daughters do that to daddies. And I feel blessed that I've become a hands-on dad for my darling daughter, Micah.

Michael Floyd Thompson

You Made Me a Daddy

To understand your parents' love, you must raise children of your own.

Chinese Proverb

It had been a long labor and things were not progressing. The first picture of our soon-to-be-born daughter was an X-ray showing the problem. Her forehead was caught on my wife's pubic bone and our daughter was trying to be born chin first.

My daughter's heart rate was steady and strong, but it was decided she would be born by C-section. My wife was saying, "This is not the way it was supposed to be." I just wanted it to be done with. Within a few minutes of the operation starting, Maria entered this world. The nurse held her up for us to see her. Her eyes were wide open and she had a look on her face that said, "What's going on here?"

The nurses cleaned up Maria and handed her to me. She was so small. Maria fit between my elbow and my hand. She had light brown hair and eyes as big as quarters. I held our daughter close to my wife, so she could see that everything was all right. Everything was all right; our daughter was here.

A few years and a few more children later, I was playing with Maria in the kitchen. I looked at her and said, "Maria, do you know what makes you so special?"

"No, what makes me special?" she asked.

"When you were born, you made me a daddy."

Apparently, that impressed her young mind. I heard her tell her friends that she made me a daddy.

That was twenty-one years ago.

Maria has become a beautiful young woman who married a kind and hardworking young man. In her, the miracle of life continues. In another few months I will be able to hold another small being. I will look that child in the eyes and say, "You know what makes you so special? You made me a grandpa!"

Douglas M. Brown

Reason to Live

My husband, Steve, was dying. He had already been in the hospital over thirty times. Many of those stays had been in the critical care unit. Even though we both spoke of his impending death, we tried not to let it steal whatever happiness we could find each day, whether it was in the hospital or at home. Steve would still try to play his guitar and write music. I didn't allow myself to think too much about what life was going to be like without him. I just kept going through the motions of everything that had to be done to care for Steve and our three children each day. It seemed like God gave me extra energy and perseverance beyond my ability to take care of everything that needed to be done.

Then I came down with flulike symptoms. I kept throwing up and was so tired I could barely move. After a couple of days, Steve suggested I might be pregnant. "No way!" *How could I be pregnant—with a dying husband, two teens, and a preschooler?*

He insisted I go to the store and get a home pregnancy test. After much stalling, I finally did. As my husband, my teen daughter, and I waited for the results, I adamantly denied the very possibility I could be pregnant. When the results showed positive, I couldn't even speak. I just held up the test for them to see the "positive." I sat down in absolute shock as Steve began cheering and hollering. I had not seen him that happy in several years. I was simply numb! Chrissy, our thirteen-year-old daughter, sarcastically said, "Way to go, Mom and Dad. Don't you know what causes that?"

As the shock slowly faded, I began with the questions. How will I ever be able to raise four kids without Steve? How can I handle more on top of what I'm already doing? We can't afford another child with all these medical expenses. What will people think of us having another baby when he's dying? Will Steve even live to see this child?

Steve could not wait to tell the world about our new baby! He wanted to announce it at church on Sunday. It wasn't even real to me yet. I was still trying to absorb it all. The news had given Steve new life and joy and reason to live. So I told him he could announce it. As Steve proudly stood up to tell the whole church his wonderful news, I just wanted to slide down in the pew and disappear. It looked like everyone was just as shocked as me, but as happy as Steve. I graciously accepted everyone's congratulations. When I got home, I decided this must be real since other people knew about it, too.

As the months passed, Steve continued having medical crises that landed him back in the hospital; his spirits, however, were lifted higher than ever at the thought of a new baby, especially after finding out it would be a boy! Even at the hospital when he saw nurses he knew, he would brag about his coming son. I don't believe I had ever seen him so proud. Perhaps it was because he had been fighting feeling useless and being a burden. By fathering a son, he had accomplished one of the greatest feats known.

He announced one day that he had chosen a name for our son. I tentatively said, "Okay?"

"His name should be Jake."

"Jake! That's an old cowboy name! No one is named Jake anymore!" (That was before almost everyone began naming their boys Jake.) I wanted to argue, but I didn't have the heart. He was so proud. Since he probably wouldn't get to be a part of his son's life, I could at least let Steve name him.

At one point during the pregnancy, Steve almost died. As I stood next to his hospital bed, Steve assured me he was not going to die until his son knew him.

The day they scheduled me to have induced labor, Steve was really sick. As the nurses gave me medication, Steve's brother was stopping by the pharmacy to bring him more of his medications. Nothing could keep him away from Jake's birth. As the pains got more intense, I struggled to stay calm, knowing that Steve was always calm through his pain. Steve held my hand as we went into the delivery room. He was extremely supportive and compassionate with me—until the baby was born. Then he completely forgot about me! He scooped up that baby and whisked him off into the other room to show him off to everyone. I heard wild cheers for the baby I hadn't yet seen!

Whatever pain and suffering Steve had earlier in the day was completely overridden by the joy of a brand-new son. I hadn't seen such a healthy-looking glow on his face in years!

When we got Jake home, Steve fed him and rocked him. He played his guitar for him. He used every moment possible to get to know his newest son. There were still more hospital stays, but Steve kept fighting to stay alive. Jake could only stay at the hospital for short visits because he would climb all over his daddy, pulling out tubes. Steve would just say, "That's okay! He's my son!" Even when Steve continued to grow more weary, his face would light up when Jake was around.

Jake was a little over two years old when his dad died quietly one morning. I was giving CPR, knowing he would not come back, when I noticed little Jake had innocently crawled up in bed to lie next to his daddy. Just as his dad had been with him when he was born, Jake was with his dad when he died.

Jake is now fifteen years old. That's the age his dad was when I first started dating him. He has curly hair and charming looks like his dad. Even more important, he acts a lot like his dad. He is friendly and outgoing. He's a happy, respectful young man. He even plays guitar—the same one his dad played. He listens to tapes of his dad's music. I think of the shock of finding out I was pregnant and I laugh now. I wouldn't trade Jake for anything! Often he surprises me with little memories he has of his dad. God helped Steve live long enough for Jake to know him!

Eva Juliuson

Better than a Sermon

Nothing I've ever done has given me more joy and reward than being a good father to my children.

Bill Cosby

My son, Brooks, was two and a half years old when I remarried. David entered my life the day my divorce was final from my first husband. I thought I had sworn off men completely, except for Brooks. Brooks was the only man for me. I was convinced that I would never find anyone who could live up to my new standards. Not to mention the standards that I had set for a stepfather; however, David's smile on our first meeting told me that he might just be that man.

Over the next two weeks, David was on my mind a lot. The fact that he attended church of his own free will and that he was thirty-nine years old and had never been close to marriage was very appealing to me. It was there, in his smile, that I melted. He had a smile that said "I will always treat you like a princess."

We soon started dating and Brooks began to go on outings with us as well. We went to the park, the pool, the zoo, and the children's museum. Then I noticed that David was changing dirty diapers and reading to my son at bedtime. David stepped into the role of father as naturally as if he had been there since the day Brooks was born.

I am happy to say that Brooks and I accepted David's proposal. We married in the fall of 2000. The father-son bond continued to grow between David and Brooks. A couple of years later we bought a house and settled in as a family together. The next step for our family was for it to grow. One Sunday when I was eight months pregnant, four-year-old Brooks tripped and fell up three concrete stairs. During that ordeal of swollen, bloody lips and gums, Brooks asked David if he could call him Daddy sometimes, "because you are like my daddy, you know."

A month later, Grace arrived in our family. David, Brooks, and Daddy were so excited. David made sure that Brooks transitioned well with his new little sister. Whenever someone came to the house to see Grace, David let Brooks have the big boy job of showing them her room. David told him also that Grace needed help opening her baby presents, and he happily obliged.

Attending church for the first time since Grace was born, David and I sat in the balcony with our four-week-old daughter so that we could make a quick exit if needed. It was the beginning of the worship service, and Grace was sleeping peacefully in her carrier, but David couldn't stand it. He had to take her out and hold her. He cradled her so lovingly that it made all the women in the choir melt. David swaddled her, held her out in front of him, and just looked at her.

For an hour, he just held Grace and watched her sleep. Toward the end of the service I glanced over and caught him smiling at her. At that very moment it hit me. His look said to Grace, *I will love you forever. I will treasure you, for you are a princess. I will provide for you all the days of your life with love, food, shelter, and clothing. I will do everything in my power to teach you the ways of the world and keep you safe.* He showered her with the same look and smile I received on the first day that we met.

Later that week, two women from the church choir shared with me how precious my husband and daughter were during Sunday worship. They said it was as if two sermons were going on that day. But David's sermon was the better of the two.

April Smith Carpenter

"Why did you wake him up early?"

Along for the Ride

Times have changed the birth experience into a family affair. A columnist in the local paper recalled a time when men weren't allowed in the delivery room as their wives birthed babies. One of the cruelest twists of fate occurred when my twin brother, Jim, and I were born. To begin with, no one, including the obstetrician, knew that my mother would deliver twins. Those were the days before ultrasound, and the doctor evidently didn't distinguish two separate heartbeats. When I came and Jim followed nine minutes later, a surprised physician stuck his head out of the delivery room door and yelled down the hall to the waiting room, "Mr. Rector, come here and see what you've done!"

These days things are much more open and relaxed. Dads no longer are banished to the wasteland of waiting rooms where they pace and chain-smoke cigarettes. My wife, Amy, and I spent the entire time in a labor room. As a dad, I became an integral part of the process as the coach for the delivery. In my great wisdom and training, I reminded Amy to breathe, to blow short bursts of breath during labor pains, and to take one final, deep cleansing breath at the end of the pain. At other times all I could do was wipe the brow of my tormented wife with a damp cloth and offer her ice chips.

Maybe I'm way out of line here, but I figure dads are useless in the labor room. All we do is offer moral support. That's little consolation to a woman who feels that her insides are being torn apart. In moments of semiconsciousness, some women have expressed their true feelings toward their husbands. In voices that eerily resemble the possessed little girl in the movie *The Exorcist*, these mothers-to-be curse their men and call upon evil spirits to inflict similar pain on their spouses. Luckily, the closest I came to any pain was nearly passing out as I forgot to breathe when Amy began to experience contractions. In fact, one nurse threatened to banish me to that godforsaken waiting room if I didn't shape up. Maybe I'd have been better off if she'd exiled me.

The labor room isn't a place for social calls. My wife was somewhere between delivering our daughter and ripping off my head when the door of the labor room swung open and in walked a perky little nurse's assistant. She stopped short, tilted her clueless head, and squealed in a teenage girl's spine-piercing voice, "Mr. Rector, what are you doing here?"

Before I could answer, my wife answered for me, metamorphosing into some kind of depraved creature that growled for this "spawn of Satan" to get out—IMMEDIATELY! Leaving was in the teen's best interest, as I was sure that Amy would have jumped from the bed and strangled the girl if she had uttered another syllable. The major lesson I learned from this is that as a high school English teacher I couldn't escape my former students, even in a room as far removed from the public as one designed for childbirth.

The delivery room was a place that brought out my squeamish side. The doctor worked as my wife pushed. I held her hand tightly and reminded her to breathe, and she kindly refrained from knocking me out. One time my eyes wandered from Amy's, and I looked into what appeared to be a gigantic rearview mirror placed above our heads. What I saw scared me witless. Some strange life-form was appearing, and it was more than I could stand as scenes from every alien movie raced through my mind. From that moment until the nurse handed Lacey Alice to me, I kept my eyes glued to those of my wife.

When I first viewed my daughter, I was concerned about her well-being. The child had penetrating blue eyes, but she was the color of an elephant. My concerns were alleviated when the nurse informed me that Lacey's color would improve dramatically after she had taken a few breaths. Sure enough, the child began to resemble a human, and I stopped worrying. At that moment, the three of us shared our first moments even though the room was crowded with a doctor and three nurses. Our awe at this newly arrived creation kept Amy and me from noticing the medical staff.

The best thing after Lacey's birth was that she and Amy stayed in the hospital for another week. My daughter was a bit jaundiced, and the staff placed her under what looked like lights used to keep burgers warm at a fast-food restaurant. I visited a couple of times each day, and we spent a few moments alone. The arrival of a child, however, was not a private affair. Sometimes the whole world seemed to be parading through the door during what should have been closed sessions. The time for being alone came later, when new parents try to figure out the right things to do.

I have loved my daughter since her birth, and her brother, Dallas, only added to our family's happiness. Yet, I want to tell every man who utters, "We're pregnant!" that he doesn't have a clue about things unless he's ready to

Customer Appreciation

Motherhood turned me into a fast-food enterprise with on-demand service, twenty-four hours a day. It didn't take long after our "grand opening" for fatigue to hit.

My husband tried to help. But there's not much a new dad can do for a nursing newborn except hold 'em between refueling and exhaust procedures.

I'd just finished refilling our eight-pound life-changer when I heard the telltale rumble of discharge. I sat limp in my rocker wondering how a sleep-deprived new mom could find the energy for what seemed like the 456th "maintenance duty" of the day.

I slogged into the nursery and laid baby Zach on a changing pad in the crib. As I reached for a fresh diaper, I spotted a note on the top one: "Zach appreciates it and so do I." Only one person could have written that.

I passed by the washer and noticed another sign: "Thanks for taking a load off our minds and our dirty bodies." It had to be the same author.

That night, as I crawled under the blanket, anticipating more exhausting night duty, another note greeted me: "I love you."

Did I say there's not much a new dad can do? I stand

corrected. A few strategic love notes lifted my flagging spirits. There's a lot to be said for the power of customer appreciation!

Jeanne Zornes

Organizing Tips

• Keep a list of ongoing items that need to get done in one location. Include the basics, such as emptying all trash bins in the house, washing the dishes, going through mail, and so on. This enables your spouse to view it on his own when he's in that supportive mode to help out.

• Keep a log of your baby's day (time of feedings, diaper changes, and so forth). This way, when your spouse is on "baby duty," you won't need to give an update and remember all the details. Your spouse can look and see when your baby was last changed and change the baby if needed.

Supportive Tips

- Let your spouse participate in taking care of your newborn. This can enhance the bonding process between them. Sometimes we're quick to jump in because we think we should, or that our spouse may not do it right. The more your spouse does, however, the better he or she will get at it.

- Spouses want to help; sometimes they're just not sure how. Write out a list of *all* the things that need to regularly get done. Include something as basic as your need to take a shower. This can give your significant other the specifics about what they can do to support you in getting your basic needs met.

6

LESSONS FROM BABY

It's not only children who grow. Parents do too. As much as we watch to see what our children do with their lives, they are watching us to see what we do with ours. I can't tell my children to reach for the sun. All I can do is reach for it, myself.

Joyce Maynard

Learning Curve

I knew the pros and cons of on-demand feeding versus feeding a baby on a schedule. I understood the different methods for burping a newborn. I was versed on the importance of reading stories and playing classical music for children, even when they were fresh out of the womb. But despite studying every parenting magazine, pamphlet, and book I could get my hands on prior to the delivery of my firstborn, Maddie, I spent the first week of her life learning things doctors, researchers, and authors never mentioned.

I learned that no designer perfume, essence, or oil could compare with the sweet intoxicating scent of a newborn's breath.

I mastered the art of balance and counterbalance with a seven-pound, three-ounce body. I figured out how to slide Maddie from a cradled position to my shoulder, so I could answer the phone or hold a fork. I became proficient at maneuvering a sleeping infant from my arms to her bassinet, without her sensing the change in location.

My mom stayed with us the first week to help with the new baby. As she folded onesies, blankets, and burp cloths, I learned that a newborn goes through more outfits in a day than Imelda Marcos goes through pairs of shoes.

The grumbles in my belly were louder than Maddie's cries when I smelled the zesty lasagna Mom was baking in the oven. I discovered that while savoring the flavors of bubbling mozzarella and tangy tomato sauce, an infant needs to nurse every couple of hours—and a nursing mommy needs to eat that often, too.

While my mom helped my husband snap pieces into place on our new Pack 'n Play, I realized I loved him even more deeply now as the father of our child, even more than when he was just my husband.

When Mom drove me to Maddie's one-week doctor appointment, the sound of my daughter's shrill screams piercing my heart taught me that shots traumatize the mother more severely than they do her child.

But my true moment of enlightenment came when my mom stood at the door with her suitcases in hand. I hugged her warm body and thanked her for all she had done that week. Then I noticed the tears in her eyes. Mom always cried when we said good-bye. I thought she was overemotional, but this time I finally comprehended why. I had a terrific relationship with my mom; I loved her and appreciated her. But now I grasped that she loved me as much as I love Maddie. As I looked from her to the little girl swaddled in my arms, I truly understood. She felt that same longing, aching, all-consuming love for me that I now felt for my own daughter.

"Now you know how much I love you," Mom said, reading my mind as only a mother could.

Laura Smith

Taking the Time

The quickest way for a parent to get a child's attention is to sit down and look comfortable.
                              Lane Olinghouse

A couple of months ago, my daughter turned one. Before she was born, I imagined all of the time we would have together—taking leisurely walks, attending story time at the library, going to weekly playgroups, and spending daily mommy-baby bonding time.

Much of my third trimester was spent fantasizing about the fun my little girl and I would have once she arrived. I carried this dream with me through the first week home with my new baby; I think the epidural made me delirious. In that first week I was determined to be superwoman, keeping a superclean house and a superclean and blissful baby.

Sure, I'd heard that you should "nap when the baby naps," but there would be time for that later. For now, I had to make sure that I was the perfect picture of Holly Homemaker. Then reality set in during week two. We were fortunate to have a baby who was a good sleeper, but Mommy was not taking advantage of this. I was exhausted, sick, and wondering whether I could even handle being a mother.

I thought if I could just get everything done, then I would have some time. I began marking days off the calendar and things off the to-do list so I would have time to spend with my daughter.

Somehow days turned into weeks that turned into months, and my infant daughter was now a full-fledged fifteen-month-old toddler.

During a recent bout with a sinus infection, contracted at a once-in-a-blue-moon playgroup no doubt, I was sitting in the doctor's office and had an epiphany. I was so bored staring at the floor while waiting for the doctor to see me, that I read the poster on the wall. It was one of those inspirational posters, the kind with a nature scene and an "ideal" that we all should aspire to. This one was titled *Vision* and read, "The future comes one day at a time; let each day be your masterpiece."

It was at that moment it hit me. In my haste to get everything done ASAP, I was missing the little moments that make life so special.

I went home that night and hugged my daughter tight. As usual, she was busy exploring the dog, her blocks, the same things she sees every day, but somehow they were just as interesting and special to her as they were the day before. I thought, *maybe I could learn a thing or two from her.*

She crawled over and handed me the same book that she always does, with a story that she would want me to read to her ten times in a row. Normally I'm exasperated by the third reading. This time I vowed to appreciate her curiosity in all the details of each page; the way she'd point to every apple on the tree before letting me turn the page and the way her face lit up each time we lifted the flap and found the doggie. I realize now that I should relish the moments we have together, my daughter cuddled up on my lap as I read her stories, because soon enough she won't want to do this with me anymore. I have come to appreciate that these are the things that matter in life. The dishes and the vacuuming can wait.

Stephanie McCarty

The Hug

The best thing to hold on to in life is each other.

Anonymous

It had been a long day already. And it was only three in the afternoon. My fourteen-month-old daughter, Lucy, was teething and we'd both been up all night and all day. Nothing I did seemed to comfort her and I was getting more frustrated, closer to my wit's end. To top it off, my husband was out of town, and the late August sun was making Lucy hot and sweaty and both of us more cranky. At the same time that my heart ached for her, my head ached for aspirin.

By four o'clock, Lucy was whimpering about losing Barney under the couch and Elmo under the chair. Having rescued her stuffed animals, I hugged and rocked her. I carried her with one arm and went back to sponging mashed peas off the kitchen's tile floor and brown bananas from the crevices in her high chair. I thought about the graduate school classes I had left when she was born. Before we had Lucy, I had sworn I'd never become one of those mothers who cleaned and cooked all day in their housecoats, their hair a mess, their feet in terry cloth slippers. But there I was, my hair looking like it had gone through the heavy heat cycle of the clothes dryer, my eyes bloodshot and puffy. I indeed was still in my bathrobe, and I hadn't showered.

Carrying Lucy, because she cried at my feet if I didn't, I sang to her as I cleaned up the kitchen, beginning with "Somewhere Over the Rainbow" and resorting to "A Hundred Bottles of Beer on the Wall." Singing seemed to work. Lucy was calm until I got to bottle eighty-eight and then she let out a small whimper, which soon developed into tears. I gave up cleaning and patted her back. She was not to be consoled and let out a wail I was sure was going to alert the police.

I took Lucy for a walk, read her *Runaway Bunny*, and tried tickling and playing our favorite games. Nothing was working. I tried singing again. Nothing. If ever I needed her to sleep, it was then. But every time I brought her near the crib in her room, she cried real tears, clutching at me, screaming "Nooooo." As much as I longed to leave her there, as much as my body told me to do so, I couldn't. I stared at blue eyes rimmed with red as I brought her back into the kitchen and knew all she needed was rest. *Sleep, darn it*, a voice screamed in my head, something I would never reveal to my friends who have children.

By five o'clock, I stooped to Barney videos and chocolate ice cream. This brought me some reprieve. I collapsed on the couch beside her and wondered if I was doing something wrong, somehow falling short as a new mother. Darkness came with me hardly noticing. I told myself that it was not a terrible thing to put my daughter to bed just a little early that night.

We climbed the stairs together, Lucy and I, her small petal fingers holding onto both my hands high above her head. She let out a sigh at the top of the steps by her bedroom. "Me too, Lucy," I said softly, picking her up. I lifted her onto the changing table, feeling more tired than I ever knew possible. I missed the wonderful glow, the bigger-than-life, stronger-than-any-words kind of love I felt for my daughter. I wasn't used to being so irritated and over-whelmed. Both of us quiet, I put Lucy's Mickey Mouse pajamas on her. Silent and somewhat still, she stood on the changing table as I held her close to zip her up. I breathed in the clean smell of her hair, feeling blond curls tickle my chin. A certain sadness tugged at me. This isn't what I thought motherhood would be. Suddenly, Lucy reached her arms around my neck, holding the back of my head tight between her arms. Little hands, little every-thing, pulled me to her and she pressed her cheek to mine. It took only a moment to realize what was happening. *She's hugging me, she's hugging me,* I wanted to shout. *She's hugging me for the very first time.* I wanted to yell for my hus-band, a neighbor, anyone to come see what my daughter was doing for the first time.

We held each other for a few seconds, my daughter standing on the changing table dressed in her fuzzy red sleeper, her arms around my neck, her cheek pressed to my left shoulder. "Oh, Lucy," I whispered, my words tight with tears. I never wanted to let go.

Lucy let go first and was onto her next discovery, ready to bed down with Piglet, Pooh, and her favorite soft blan-ket. I stood next to the crib, looking down at her. She was so beautiful lying there, holding Pooh, blinking blue jew-els at me. I stroked her forehead as I do each night and pulled the blanket up to her chin. As I left her room, my time now all to myself, precious solitude didn't seem quite as important, and the fatigue drifted from my shoulders. I was preoccupied with her very first hug and how lucky I was to have gotten it.

Martine Ehrenclou

"So who do you think Mom will housebreak first?
Me or you?"

The Defining Moment

People who say they sleep like a baby usually don't have one.

Leo J. Burke

"Stop crying, please stop crying," I begged my new baby. Tears of fatigue and frustration ran down my face. I had been up for hours—no weeks, actually—weeks of little sleep or rest, trying to calm my little girl. I called friends, new moms, experienced moms, and grandmas, and listened to their "tried and true" cures for a colicky baby. Nothing worked.

My new daughter had been born two-and-a-half weeks early. She had a "premature suck," the inability to feed properly. I wasn't able to nurse her because my milk failed to come in, so I was bottle-feeding her. She lacked the strength and stamina to suck hard enough and long enough to get any significant amount of formula. I enlarged the hole in the nipple of the bottle, allowing the formula to flow more easily, but after a few minutes she fell asleep. The doctor put us on a rigorous schedule: wake her up by dabbing her with a cold, wet washcloth and then force-feed her, keeping her awake until she took enough liquid nourishment. We started implementing this procedure every two hours and over the course of a week progressed to every four hours. By then she managed to take almost two ounces with each feeding. Never mind that it took a good hour for her to drink two ounces. The doctor said if she didn't gain any weight by her next visit, he might classify her as a "failure to thrive" baby. And I would classify myself as a failure of a mother.

Colicky and hungry, her incessant crying and discomfort wore on my nerves. A change of formula helped a little, but not much. My arms ached from holding her. I had held her against my shoulder, stretched out in my arms, wrapped in a blanket, and even hauled her around in a baby carrier. Nothing worked, not even tummy rubs. The only things that offered any relief were the baby swing and walks in the stroller. Thank God for whoever invented baby swings and strollers.

But how long can one really leave a baby in a swing? How much time could we spend taking stroller walks around our apartment complex?

So here I was, holding her, pacing, crying, both of us exhausted and inconsolable.

"Please," I begged her. "Please stop crying." As my frustration increased, her crying intensified. As she became more distressed, I felt my frustration turn to anger, to rage.

"Stop crying!" I screamed at her. And she did.

I held her in my arms, shocked at my own behavior. Her sweet little face turned to me. Our eyes met, and I knew I was out of control. I placed her delicately in her bassinet, afraid to hold her any longer. I sat down, buried my head in my hands, and sobbed.

I took a deep breath and turned to look at her lying in her bassinet, afraid to pick her up. *Who was that person who had screamed at my innocent baby?* I gazed at her little body, her tiny hands, her bald head. At that moment, all the memories of the difficulties I had gone through with my own mother surfaced and raced through my mind like a torrent of floodwaters. I reached out to my baby, stroked her arm, touched those precious baby fingers.

"I never felt loved by my own mother," I said through tears. "Looking at you here so tiny, so dependent, I can't fathom how my mother couldn't love me then and how she still can't love me. You're so fragile, so helpless. You need me. How could my mom not see that? Wasn't I a small, innocent baby like you once?"

My own pain was reflected in my child's need for me to step up, to be better, to be the adult, to be the caregiver, the nurturer, to be a mom.

"I promise to be better. I promise to put you first. I promise to be a good mom to you," I said as I picked her up and cradled her in my arms.

She remained a colicky baby. There was no miracle cure. There were days when my husband came home from work only to find us both crying. But I had changed. It was my responsibility to keep my anger and frustration in check, to provide a safe and loving environment for my child. And I did just that.

Many times in raising my children I have had to stop and think about how to parent. Many times I have had to stop and count to ten. Many times I have had to say, "Can we talk about this later?" Countless times I have had to decide if a disagreement merited a battle. And I'm sure there will be more times when I have to reevaluate my parenting strategy. But I'll embrace these times as they come, because I'm a mom.

N. Engler

Not Just Another Pretty Face

*Charm is deceptive, and beauty is fleeting; but
a woman who fears the Lord is to be praised.*

Proverbs 31:30

Since the day she was born, people have commented that our daughter Micah is a pretty baby. Being a first-time mom, I figured they were just being nice. After all, isn't it the polite response when viewing someone else's offspring?

When she was just a few hours old, one of the nurses at the hospital remarked that Micah was beautiful.

"I bet you say that about all the babies," I declared with a laugh.

"Oh, no," she replied with a serious gaze. "Most new-borns are not pretty. They have misshapened heads and squished faces without a defined chin."

I looked at my petite infant lying in the bassinet beside my hospital bed. Her head was round, her face a perfect oval. Her almond-shaped eyes weren't swollen. She had classic "Gerber baby" features.

A few weeks later, Micah accompanied me to my doctor's appointment.

"What a beautiful baby!" exclaimed the attendant.

"Thank you," I said with pride. So many people had mentioned Micah's appearance in recent weeks that now I was beginning to take credit for the way my daughter looked.

The examination room wall was covered with hundreds of pictures of new arrivals. As I waited for the doctor, I compared Micah to other newborns. Now convinced that I had given birth to the most beautiful and perfect baby, I agreed when the doctor entered the room and said that Micah was pretty.

The next day, my mother came by to watch Micah while I ran some errands. As I was leaving, I waved good-bye to Micah.

"Bye-bye beautiful baby," I called to my daughter.

When I returned home, I greeted my infant.

"Hello, pretty baby," I said, bending to kiss her cheek as she lay in the crib.

Reaching over to hug my mom, I noticed a sour look on her face. "You know, it's really not enough to be beautiful," my mom interrupted. "Micah has nothing to do with the way she looks. Instead of telling her how pretty she is, she needs affirmations that encourage her spirit."

Then Mom looked at Micah and said, "What a kind and loving baby you are."

Since then, I've been telling little Micah that she is smart, caring, patient, considerate, and obedient. Some people may think it's crazy to talk to an infant in this manner, but I want to get in the habit of validating Micah so when she is old enough to understand the meaning behind the words, she'll know what traits are most important to her family.

Stephanie Welcher Thompson

Motherhood: How It Feels
to Feel Everything

I became a mother at twenty-two. I was fresh out of college, married a year, and looking for a way out of teaching squirmy eighth graders the fine points of grammar—back in the days when pregnant teachers weren't particularly welcome in classrooms.

What was I thinking? My husband and I barely knew what marriage was about, let alone the enormity of taking on the most important work of our lives. Ah, youth!

From the moment we brought Jill home from the hospital to our little Cape Cod house, everything I thought I knew about the world changed. Nothing could have prepared me for this permanent assignment. Parenthood is, after all, a learn-by-doing, seat-of-the-pants proposition much of the time. And rest assured that back then, there were no Internet sites or chat rooms, no parenting groups, no hotlines for support.

There was Doctor Spock, and if you were lucky, there were older relatives from whom to borrow great stashes of wisdom. But generally, new motherhood was like facing a

final exam every day in a subject in which one was woefully unprepared.

The first time Jill screamed all night from an undiag-
nosed earache, I thought I would surely perish. The sound
of her howls pierced something in me that I hadn't known
was there. Her pain, which I couldn't stop, consumed me
and taught me that when you are a mother, you're never
again free from guilt.

This was loving of a different order—surreal, enveloping,
almost terrifying in its intensity. I figured it couldn't be as
extreme the second and third times around. I was wrong.

Being a mother has made me the most vulnerable of
creatures. Friends assured me that they, too, felt a helplessness that defied mere words; that they, too, trembled
or wept the first time a spunky little creature walked off in
that crooked kindergarten line, never looking back, or
rode off on a two-wheeler bike into the wind—and into
the world.

I learned very quickly, and very young, that you never
have so much to lose as when you give your heart to a
child. Kids humble you and make you crazy and angry
and worried and overjoyed, sometimes all at once. They
remind you that fancy degrees and presumed wisdom
aside, there are questions you'll never be able to answer
about God and death and sex and sincerity.

And anytime I thought I'd finally mastered all the steps
of the intricate mother-daughter ballet, Jill or Amy or
Nancy would ambush me with an unexpected emotional
plié or arabesque, and I'd be down for the count. I think of
the times we retreated into our separate corners to nurse
our wounds, of the tears shed and the doors slammed shut
and the angry words hurled. But then, somehow, we
always found our way back into each other's hearts, blind-
sided by the ferocity of feelings but still needing one
another.

Our daughters are all grown women now. So I've already been through the impossible angst of three adolescences, three good-byes on college campuses that ripped my heart out, three graduations, too many painful love affairs, and trips to dangerous places. And given all that, if I could negotiate a deal with God to do it all again, I absolutely would. Only better.

All of my daughters are mothers themselves now, learning firsthand what blind daring it takes to assume that role. Now it's their turn to live the dizzying extremes and built-in contradictions of motherhood.

And I suspect that when they look into the faces of their children, they will be reminded again of the unnerving helplessness, the giddy shock of blinding love, and the impossible demands and delicious rewards of motherhood.

In other words, as someone once observed, how it feels to feel everything. Because that, after all, is what being a mother is really all about.

Sally Friedman

Organizing Tips

- Even if you're not innately organized, the process inevitably happens due to the needs of babies. But to get a jump-start, try to establish a "home" for all your essential items. When rushing about, it's best to keep your keys, umbrella, jacket, diaper bag, and other things in the same place every time.

- Because of the numerous details involved in taking care of our little ones, using a to-do list can make a profound difference. Consider organizing your list with three columns—one for phone calls, another for e-mails, and the third for other "to-dos."

- If your baby has a favorite blanket or bear, consider buying a few of them in case one gets lost or needs to be washed.

- When you have many items that need to be completed, learn to prioritize. Take baby steps. Schedule by breaking down your morning, afternoon, and evening rather than the entire day all at once. This can be overwhelming on an hourly or daily basis.

7

MOTHERHOOD

1A

*When you are a mother, you are never really
alone in your thoughts. A mother always
has to think twice, once for herself and
once for her child.*

Sophia Loren, Women and Beauty

A Legacy of Love

Please just go to sleep, I silently begged the small pink bundle cradled in my lap. The old wooden rocking chair, creaking endlessly against the floorboards, seemed to work against my best efforts to get my infant daughter (and myself) some much-needed rest. Standing up, I tried a new position, this time swaddling my daughter in her fuzzy blanket and holding her close to my chest. Her squirms and gurgles did nothing to reassure me that this would be an easy night. Mockingly, the digital clock flipped to 3:00 AM. An overflowing laundry basket stared menacingly from the corner of the room.

I tried it all—nursing, rocking, and even several different types of pacifiers, which were promptly spit right back in my general direction—thank you very much. Exhaustion overwhelmed me as tears flowed, this time from me, the mother, the supposedly competent adult.

Big blue eyes stared up at me as the clock slowly ticked forward. *Why can't this be easier? All I want to do is sleep.* Looking around the room for something to get my mind off this seemingly endless night, I spotted the blue and pink patchwork quilt hanging on the nursery wall.

My grandmother wanted me to have a baby quilt and

began her stitches before I was even pregnant. At age eighty-eight, Grammie sensed that time was of the essence. I smiled as I counted seventeen hand-sewn calico hearts. *These are blocks full of love,* I thought to myself. Somehow I felt my grandmother's presence as I looked up at the quilt she had made for my daughter.

Grammie rocked seven babies and never complained. She raised a set of twins when she only had clothes and supplies for one child. Her baby boy died in infancy. *I can do this. Just have patience, like Grammie.*

Looking up at the quilt, my memories took me back to childhood visits to my grandmother's western Pennsylvania farm. A one-lane gravel road led to the two-hundred-year-old farmhouse where Grammie always welcomed me with a big kiss and soft sugar cookie, complete with raisin eyes, nose, and smile. Inhaling, I once again smelled the comforting scents of a farm summer: freshly baled hay, sweet, garden-fresh tomatoes, and mint leaves picked for a refreshing drink of tea. This was a good place, a homestead for our family for generations.

Closing my eyes, I could hear the familiar swish-swish of cows' tails shooing away flies in the barn. I could see Grammie, busy washing milkers for the dairy cows each morning, taking time out to open the milk tank, showing me the swirling gallons ready to be sent to the local dairy. She involved me in all of the farm chores, from hoeing weeds to picking garden vegetables for supper. "I am not a very fast bean-picker," I commented, noticing my near-empty basket. "Every bean you pick is one I don't have to," she said, smiling. "You are Grandma's good helper."

Stepping into the farmhouse, I could smell the yeast rising on a miniature loaf of bread Grammie had made just for me. "Just pinch off the dough between your fingers," she instructed, helping me make homemade rolls and egg noodles. When I mistakenly turned the oven to "broil" instead of "bake," she told me, "Elderberry pie always tastes better with a scoop of vanilla ice cream on it anyway."

Reaching up to touch the many careful stitches on my baby's quilt, I remembered afternoons spent sewing with Grammie. A thimble on my thumb, again I was an eight-year-old girl learning how to sew patchwork squares into blankets for my dolls. Colorful fabrics and pattern books covered the wooden dining room table, evidence of Grammie's other projects put on hold. Our time spent together was precious—time to thread a needle, talk, and feel the love between generations.

Standing now as a young mother looking at the quilt above my baby's crib, I am ashamed of my selfish thoughts. *Why in the world am I crying? Sure, this is a rough night, but I have a perfectly healthy baby and all the time in the world to love and comfort her. This night won't last forever, so I'd better take it all in—baby powder smells, cuddly closeness, and ten tiny fingers wrapped around mine.*

Feeling the supportive spirit of my grandmother, I bent down and kissed my baby's soft cheek. A quilt covered in hearts reminded me of all that is really important in life. Sh-h-h, my child, a grandmother's legacy of love will see us through this long night.

Stefanie Wass

In All Seriousness

Sarah said, "God has brought me laughter, and everyone who hears about this will laugh with me."
Genesis 21:6

Life was serious. There were goals to accomplish and I was a goal-oriented person. Even in pregnancy, I was well prepared. The details of my job were looked after, cloth diapers were ready, little sleepers were neatly folded in a dresser in a room that was waiting for its new inhabitant. I was going to do parenting just right, according to schedule. That was my goal.

"What will I do with my spare time?" I lamented to my mother-in-law as we sat chatting about my pending maternity leave in less than two months. A blank look flitted across her face, she hesitated, and then quickly changed the subject. *I wonder what she was going to say,* I thought.

Time passed and after a two-week hospital stay, a long day of induced labor, and one C-section later, I held an absolute delight in my shaking hands. Alyssa GraceAnn, six pounds, five ounces.

The next morning, a nurse bustled into my room carrying a bundle and cheerily announced, "Mrs. Wooldridge, it is time to feed your baby." *Baby?* It took a moment for my anesthetic-dulled mind to understand that our lives had drastically changed in the past twelve hours.

When we arrived home, I quickly realized that the ideal, serious picture I had imagined before baby was totally different from reality. Cloth diapers were tossed into the back of the closet and my husband brought home Pampers as I thanked God for the miracle of modern living. The enlightening parenting books I had carefully chosen were filed in the "read on a need-to-know basis" section of my bookcase. My husband developed the skill of "reading women." If he arrived home and neither of us was crying, he entered farther.

At one point, I vividly remembered my mother-in-law's blank look, and I loved her all the more for her silence at my innocence. She knew.

The six-week postsurgery date was quickly approaching and I felt it was a day to celebrate. Alyssa and I were getting on a schedule that was workable, and I was feeling more confident in my mothering skills. I decided to take her downtown the following day to enjoy the fall weather and do a little shopping.

The next morning dawned beautiful. The air was crisp, and the leaves were turning striking shades of red and orange. With excitement and anticipation, I dressed my after-baby-body in a loose top and stretchy pants. I consoled myself with the thought that my daughter would be the focus of attention.

I got us both dressed and in the car and drove downtown. Success! I slid some coins in the parking meter and then painstakingly poked and pulled and adjusted just about everything to get the baby in a front baby carrier. Off we went. It felt great! There was a bounce in my step as I relished the feeling of being a young, capable mother. I thought every person I met thought so too as they walked past us and smiled. I gamely smiled back. People sure were friendly to new moms.

After walking around the stores for an hour or so, I figured I had just enough time to get home precisely when the baby would need to be fed. I headed back to the car.

I glanced sideways in a store window to get a glimpse of a mom with her baby enjoying a carefree day together. It was with shock and embarrassment I realized that my pants were obviously on backward!

That moment was monumental in my journey into parenthood. It was the day I learned how to laugh. Loud. At myself. This serious, no-nonsense mom went home a little lighter in spirit, more relaxed, and with a new sense of humor. I was more confident, not so much in my super-abilities and coping skills, but in the realization that although life may not turn out exactly as I had planned, it would turn out. It was the start of letting some things go and, in the process, enjoying the journey a whole lot more.

Several years later I was sitting with a friend who was expecting her first baby. I listened to her as she mused about all the free time she would have on her upcoming maternity leave. "Isn't it wonderful?" she asked. I considered telling her about all-nighters and the bone-weary daze that accompanies them, or the feeling of being totally responsible for another human being, or desiring moments of quiet to think or take a bath or comb your hair and put makeup on in the same morning. I considered telling her that the payoff was a look from your child that takes your breath away because of its beauty, of watching your husband and loving him even more because of his care and concern for you both. I looked at her, I hesitated, and then I changed the

The Good Enough Mother

All that I am or ever hope to be, I owe to my angel Mother.

Abraham Lincoln

"I'm tired, the house is a wreck, and I haven't opened the mail all week," I complained to my mother on the telephone.

Micah was three months old and my once perfectly ordered life was more disorganized than ever. I assumed taking care of a newborn would be challenging, but I never dreamed how time-consuming it would be. Balancing marriage and motherhood with running a household, writing a newspaper column, and producing a weekend radio program had me sneaking out of bed at midnight to work or clean house into the morning hours. Friends said it would get easier, but I seemed to get further behind each day.

"Let Michael help you," she suggested, not knowing that my husband already emptied the trash and vacuumed for me.

"Well, he does what he can," I whined.

"Then, let me help," offered Mom. "You work at home, so I'll come over and watch Micah during the day until you get caught up."

It sounded like a great idea and Mom began coming over every afternoon. After a few weeks, things were still scattered.

"Why can't I catch up?" I asked Mom.

"You're always busy when I'm here," she replied. "I can't figure out why you're not making more progress."

That afternoon while Micah slept, Mom tiptoed into the kitchen. She unloaded the dishwasher, then reloaded it with the dishes stacked in the sink.

After a telephone interview, I came out of my office for a glass of tea. Reaching into the cabinet, I noticed the glasses weren't positioned the way I normally arranged them. I moved them to their proper places. Pulling out a drawer for a spoon to sugar my tea, I saw the silverware was not aligned, so I straightened it. After stirring my tea, I put the spoon in the dishwasher and spied a trace of ketchup on a plate. I took all the dishes out and began scrubbing them.

"What are you doing?" asked Mom. "I already rinsed those."

"I know, thank you, but there was a bit of food on one of the dishes," I explained.

"So you're taking them all out of the dishwasher and rerinsing them?" she challenged, her eyebrows raised.

I smiled meekly.

A few days later, Michael had some extra time before work and took a load of laundry out of the dryer, folded it, and left it on the couch. When Mom came over to babysit, she caught me refolding each item.

"Why are you doing that?" she asked.

"Michael doesn't fold things the way I do," I explained.

"What difference does it make?" asked Mom.

"I like it done perfectly," I replied.

Later that afternoon, I returned home from an appointment. Mom and Micah were playing on a quilt in the living room.

"How's my baby girl?" I lifted Micah and started to kiss her face when I noticed dried milk on her shirt.

"Didn't you see she spit up?" I asked.

"Yes, it was just a little and I wiped it with her burp cloth," replied Mom.

"I always change her if she drools or spits up," I said.

"And, honey, how many times a day do you change her clothes?" Mom asked.

"Four or five," I said.

Mom wrinkled her brow. I knew she didn't understand.

"She's so cute and I just want her to look perfect all the time," I explained.

Mom looked me in the eye.

"Honey, I want to talk to you about something," she began. "I've been watching you these past few weeks and I think I know why you are always behind."

This was music to my ears. Obviously, she solved the mystery. I was excited to hear her solution.

"You want everything to be done perfectly."

I waited for her to say more.

"Of course," I replied. "Doesn't everyone?"

"The problem is not that you have too much to do, but that you want it done a certain way. Not everything needs to be done perfectly," she said. "It takes too much time, plus when children grow up with parents who expect perfection, they feel criticized."

Now Mom had my attention. Micah was a sweet baby. I didn't want to do anything to hurt or stifle my daughter.

Then Mom told me the story about the Good Enough Mother.

The Good Enough Mother asked her son to make his

bed. The boy struggled to pull up the sheets and bed-spread. Finally finished, he felt a great sense of accomplishment and ran to tell his mother.

When the mother went into his room, she noticed that the pillow was lopsided and the stripes on the bedspread weren't straight.

"What do you think?" he asked.

She patted him on the head and said, "Well done, son."

"But, Mother, I couldn't match up the stripes perfectly," said the boy.

"You're right, son," she said. "It's not perfect, but it's good enough."

The next day her son was coloring a picture. It was difficult to stay within the lines. He showed the Good Enough Mother the paper.

"What do you think?" he asked.

The Good Enough Mother looked at the green dog and purple grass. She patted her son on the head and said, "Well done, son."

"But, Mother, I couldn't stay perfectly within the lines," said the boy.

"You're right son," she said. "It's not perfect, but it's good enough."

Then my mother put her hand around my shoulder.

"Most tasks don't need to be done perfectly. Doing things good enough is just that—good enough!" she said with a smile.

I went into my office. As I sat in my executive chair, I reflected on the story and looked at the file folders stacked on my desk. I'd not put them in drawers because I wanted to buy a label maker and hadn't found one on sale for the past year.

A few minutes later, Mom walked through the doorway.

"What are you doing?" she asked.

"I'm writing the subject on these files and putting them

away." I said. "It's not the way I originally wanted to do it, but now I realize, it's good enough."

These days, when I catch myself procrastinating on completing duties or taking too much time trying to do things perfectly, I remember the story of the Good Enough Mother. Everything doesn't have to be perfect, just good enough!

Stephanie Welcher Thompson

"It's a new workout video. It shows a mother chasing
after three little children all day."

I'm a Mess

I am a mess. Strained carrots are smeared on my right shoulder, mashed pears on my left. Somewhere behind me is a dribble of spit-up, generously deposited by a well-fed infant. I'm a walking food collage.

My hair is freshly washed and dried, though I haven't had time to use my blow-dryer in ages. I've found it easier to hang my head out the van window on the morning car-pool run. My curling iron is heating up. It's been heating up for three days. It's probably hot. I plan to use it when I get a spare minute. The lists of things I plan to do when I get a spare minute fills a three-ring binder.

Yep, I'm a mess. I'm wearing leggings that contain Lycra and spandex. They are black. I wear black frequently since the birth of my fourth child. Unfortunately, there's not enough black spandex in the world to return my shape to its pre-pregnancy dimensions.

My makeup seems to last a long time now. I'm sure this is the same bottle of foundation I had when my first son was born. It's probably time to trade "Dewy Fresh" for "Desperately Frazzled." My lipstick is melting on the dash of the minivan. It's easier to use that way. I just swipe my finger across it on my way into the store. My husband likes the natural look. Just like he preferred natural birth control.

At least I'm wearing shoes. I have to wear them for medical reasons. My doctor has refused to surgically remove any more Legos from the bottom of my feet.

I'm a mess all right. I slump down on the sofa—well, the floor, actually. With my hair hanging in my eyes, it's easy to misjudge distances. The baby waves his tiny fists at me, glad to have me at his level.

The front door slams and thudding footsteps skid to a stop in front of me. It's a boy. His dirty, untied sneakers, holey jeans, and wild "bed-head" lead me to believe he must belong to me. He bends down and throws his scrawny arms around me. His unaccustomed, spontaneous affection startles me.

"Thank you, sweetie!" I say, as he gets up to run off again. "What was that for?"

"It's 'cause you look so prettyful sitting there on the floor," he says, and the door bangs shut behind him.

Sure, I'm a mess. But all the beauty products in the world can't reproduce the glow on my face, put there by a scruffy little boy who thinks I'm prettyful.

Cindy Hval

The Only Mother on Campus

During my second month of graduate school, I learned that I was pregnant. I was in shock. My husband and I had only lived in the area for two months. We hadn't even unpacked our boxes. Knowing no one else, I called my advisor at home, prefacing my question by mentioning that I had an odd request. Then I just blurted it out.

"Can you recommend an obstetrician?"

It was very quiet on the other end of the line. Finally, my advisor spoke.

"I'll go get my wife."

That was the start of my strange and wonderful experience of pregnancy in graduate school. My first semester of classes was a whirlwind. I survived my load of coursework with an extension on one project. My next semester covered my second and part of my third trimesters, so I opted to attend school part-time.

Being pregnant in a college setting was a weird experience. I didn't know anyone else in my situation. Hoping to find a sense of kinship, I visited the Women's Center on campus. Searching the shelves of the small library I found there, I noticed more titles about abortion than pregnancy. As I walked back across campus, I took a closer look at the

other students. *Had I ever seen another pregnant woman on
campus?* Other than me, there were no pregnant students
in any of my classes.

Late in my pregnancy, my classmates surprised me
with a traditional baby shower, complete with gifts and
cake. I treasured the sense of fellowship, but I still felt
lonely. Many of my classmates were going away for the
summer on internships that would complete their master's projects. I jokingly referred to my summer plans as
"the baby project."

My son was thoughtful enough to be born during summer break, so I started back to classes the following fall.
Nothing was easy. I was the only student I knew who had
to take breaks from studying to breast-feed. No one else
seemed to notice that there wasn't a diaper-changing station in the entire building.

Still a part-time student, I did my best to juggle class
projects and exams while caring for my son. Two more
years passed. My old friends graduated without me; new
friends took their places. I managed to complete my master's project without the traditional internship; I couldn't
bear to spend that much time away from my son.

Finally, three years into my one-year program, it was
my turn to graduate. I remember standing with thousands
of other students on the football field in my black cap and
gown, sweltering under the hot sun. The speeches were
long and numerous, and I was distracted, wishing for a
cold drink. Then a new speaker stepped up to the podium.

"I want to take the time today to recognize those of you
who are mothers. If you are a mother, please stand."

Embarrassed, I stood up slowly. At first, I noticed that I
was the only one to rise within my group of classmates.
Then I looked across the football field and into the stands.
I was standing with hundreds of other mothers: graduat-
ing students like me, professors, grandmothers, and moth-

ers like mine, eagerly watching their babies graduate. Tears filled my eyes. I was not the only mother on campus.

As the speaker continued, I felt a unique sense of completion. In three years of school, I had earned a master's degree and brought a new life into the world. It was only fitting that I should graduate on Mother's Day.

Julie Bloss Kelsey

"Motherhood is wearing me out!"

Other Duties as Required

"Mom, have you seen my other shoe?"

"No, where did you find that one?" I asked, knowing full well that the location of the shoe in my son's hand probably had nothing to do with the spot where its elusive mate was hiding.

"In the laundry basket," my son replied.

In the laundry basket? Please tell me it's not the clean laundry.

"Did you look there for the other one?"

"Of course," my son said in his "do you really think I'm that stupid?" tone.

Hey, I'm not the one who left his shoe in a laundry basket. Of course, in our house, he might not be the guilty party either. *What am I, anyway? A detective?*

Well, yes. I am the finder of lost things. I also solve great mysteries:

"Who wrote on my antique bench?"

"How did my silver ladle get out in the garden?"

"Why are you wearing one red and one purple sock?"

Who would have thought that when I became a mother it would be so complicated? The job description might have read: *This person is responsible for the physical, social, and moral development of a child. She will provide love, care, guidance, and other duties as required.*

"What do you want to be when you grow up?" adults would ask when I was a child.

"A teacher," I had replied. I never mentioned being a mother. I had crossed that "job" off the list when I found out about the pain of childbirth.

I became a teacher. I just don't get paid. My job includes teaching basics like language development, reading appreciation, mathematical manipulation, and moral development, as well as the finer points of tic-tac-toe.

Other career paths I briefly considered were those of nurse and doctor. But frankly, I didn't like taking care of sick people. Who does? It didn't take having a child throwing up in my lap too many times for me to realize I am a nurse, too. My duties include properly diagnosing and treating a sick child. I also need to know when to call in a professional:

"So, Mrs. Dean, what seems to be wrong with your child today," the phone nurse asked.

"He has a headache, sore throat, and he just threw up on my shoe," I replied.

"What about a fever?"

"Let me check," I said as I dragged the phone over to where my son was moaning and placed my hand to his forehead. "According to the 'mommy method,' I'd say he has a fever of about 100 degrees." While doctors dismiss the accuracy of this measurement, it seems to work well enough for me. In fact, my research bears out that it works!

"Could be strep, you'd better bring him in for a culture."

I *knew* she was going to say that!

A job I never, ever considered was that of bug catcher. I don't like bugs. Now, in my head I know those little critters won't hurt me, but when I see one, instinct takes over. I just want to put as much distance between the bug and me as is possible. That goes double for spiders. So imagine my dismay when my daughter screamed out in terror:

"A spider, Mommy, a spider! He's coming closer!"

Bravely, I ran to save my daughter. A gigantic spider the size of a shriveled raisin leered at us from the corner.

"Okay darling, I'll get him." I grabbed a plastic cup and quickly placed it over the huge monster. Then, ingeniously, I slid a piece of paper under the lip of the cup, trapping the horrifying creature inside. As my daughter opened the front door, I flung the capsule with the despised arachnid into the yard. Safe at last.

One subject I did choose to study was marketing. But I never expected I'd need to use what I learned on my own children. But part of being a mom is knowing how to market a product:

"Do you want hot dogs and beans for lunch?" I asked my son.

"No, no, no," my preschooler replied. "I don't like them."

Sure you do, I thought. "Well, how about beanie weenies, then?"

My son nodded in agreement.

In addition to these jobs, I also act as a chauffeur, maid, short-order cook, guidance counselor—the list is endless. No wonder the job description says "and other duties as required." If God listed them all, who would take the job? And although I stepped into this position blindly like every other mother, I wouldn't trade it for any other job in the world.

Lynn Dean

Under New Management

You delay childbearing to advance your career and then, as soon as you give birth, you look into your baby's eyes and want to quit work. Forget that beautiful wardrobe you invested in over the years. After a baby, you won't fit into it anyway. The only thing you'll fit into is the closet. All you need is an old pair of sweats. Instead of suits, you'll wear a spit-up cloth and a nose wiper, if you're fortunate. Otherwise, you're walking toilet paper.

Coats? Shoes? Forget those. The nearest you'll get to the outdoors is the refrigerator. Before, you wouldn't dare snack while standing, but now it's as comfortable as the elastic-waistband pajamas you're still wearing at lunchtime.

Feed baby. Burp baby. Clean baby. Change diaper. Repeat. Whatever time is left over is devoted to the car seat: installation, reinstallation, loosening the straps, and tightening the straps. You will feel proud of the effort you spend in the name of safety, until your car seat is recalled for missing parts.

Instead of dumbbells at the fitness center, you lift a twelve-pound infant. Add the car seat to your reps, and your biceps will crush baby food jars. Sleep? Think fragmented intervals. Think short. Think, if you still can.

Your perspective changes. Now you see the world from the floor. You will be on your hands and knees changing diapers, cleaning up the splat mat, and picking up the most recently flung rattle or bottle. The "Mozart Effect" refers to the fact that you can no longer take a step in your home without tripping on a plastic, battery-operated toy that emits classical music, supposedly to make your tot smarter.

At this job, night school is required and classes begin at midnight. You'll learn the ins and outs of high chairs, bouncy seats, and swing sets. With a quick glance, you will discern the Baby Bjorn from the Snugli front carrier and calculate the price differential. Along the way, you will acquire a knowledge base on baby-proofing a home and develop skills in manual assembly, ranging all the way from sippy cups to portable cribs.

Without realizing it, your vocabulary changes to "boo-boo" and "choo-choo." You will instinctively begin S-P-E-L-L-I-N-G certain words. The skill sets you cultivated at work will get you nowhere now. Can you make funny sounds or wiggle your ears? That's what earns brownie points with your new boss.

There are perks, of course. You don't have to commute far to this job and you can throw away the alarm clocks, because your baby serves as an indoor rooster. Try patting his head for ten minutes of snoozing and he will laugh heartily because it's playtime. No need to bathe, brush, dress, or make coffee. Your baby is R-E-A-D-Y.

Some things won't surprise you anymore, such as watching an adult pick up a small child at the supermarket and sniff his behind. You, however, won't need to get that close.

Forget about the high-pressured decisions you made at work because deciding between the ladybug, the bumblebee, or the chili pepper Halloween costumes will have you stumped. You'll sweat over choosing between the birthday bear plates or the zoo plates.

Now you will hear yourself calling across the playground to find out where to buy those sneakers with the Velcro straps in size two. Before you were afraid to try skydiving, bungee jumping, or parasailing. None of those seem like a big deal compared with the terror of leaving your child with a babysitter. Walking out the door will feel like walking straight off a cliff.

The Parents Union Local 429 has drafted you. The dues are steep, but membership is forever. The benefits are right in front of you in your wriggly-squiggly-giggly worm, that cuddly-inchy-squinchy sweetpea, who knows no greater happiness than just to be with you.

In this job, you don't look forward to retirement.

Elizabeth Kann

Last But Not Least

My younger sister and her husband are expecting their second child, so I've been looking for a baby gift. I've always liked those books of "baby's firsts," page after fill-in-the-blank page, each bordered with teddy bears, choo-choos, or balloons. I like the way the text invites parents to record, for all time, the date of baby's first smile and first steps, first words and first bumpy-edged tooth.

But as the mother of a daughter, twelve, and a son, "almost ten," I've become aware of another kind of book that doesn't exist. And should. But never will. The Book of Lasts. It would be a place to magically keep track of all those milestones that pass without anyone realizing it. The moments we don't even think of as precious until they're gone. Those brief eras in a family that quietly shuffle out of sight like a kid in fuzzy-footed PJs.

I experienced one of those "lasts" a while back, though I didn't know it at the time. And I only realized it the other night around 3:00 AM. Our daughter, Anne, whom I had tucked in earlier, walked into our bedroom and woke me up with a whispered, "Hi, Mom." This wasn't a case of her having a bad dream or a rising fever or a middle-of-the-night fear of that gnarly-fingered, hairy-armed creature that resides between children's box springs and dust ruffles. No, for reasons that made a dreamlike sense only because it was three in the morning, she'd simply come over to say "hello" and spend some quality time with us. My eyes fluttered open. I mumbled a greeting, rolled over, and fell back to sleep. Anne did, too, without bothering to head back to her room.

So I woke up a short time later, wedged between a very sound asleep husband and a snoozing, deadweight daughter who had developed what seemed like an excess of elbows. It was time to carry Anne back to her bed where she belonged. I got up, slid my arms beneath her, and tried to lift. No go. Nothing. It was impossible. And I could no sooner scoop her up and trot down the hall than I could arm wrestle an alligator. The little girl I used to easily hoist on my hip or bounce in my arms was gone. In her place was a midsized person with size-eight feet.

Sometime, somewhere, on a day I don't remember, I had carried Anne for the last time. On that particular day, when I set her down, I had no way of knowing it was forever.

Other lost moments belong in my Book of Lasts. Like the last time my little boy, fresh from a bubble bath, said, "Warm me up, Mommy," and I folded my arms in a terry cloth hug around a pink and steaming toddler. Once this was one of our rituals. An everyday thing. Then one day, without a word, he began toweling off himself and dashing to his room so no one would see his Scooby-Doo underwear.

I never knew those were the last days, until now. I never knew I was changing the last diaper; I wasn't aware of the last afternoon nap. There was also the last time either of the kids drew a picture of me in the style of all early artists—a likeness with no neck or torso, just pairs of reedy arms and legs shooting directly out of a potato-shaped head. If I'd known no more of this genre would appear, I might have framed the last one, or at least left it hanging a while longer on the refrigerator door.

Each phase we're in, while we are in it, tricks us into believing that's how things will always be. There are days right now when I'm convinced I'll always be reminding kids in the car pool to buckle their seat belts. Always be answering the phone and saying, "Anne, it's for you." Always be looking for new containers for my son's latest catch of bugs or lizards or ribbony grass snakes. I carry the illusion that every Christmas season we'll polish off at least one box of candy canes around here. And every Fourth of July, my husband and I will sit with two kids who clap and cheer at fireworks as if the night sky could hear them.

But I'm beginning to see that today's moments are just that: today's. And tomorrow or next week or next year, these small touchstones will make their way without fuss or fanfare into my mind's revolving files of lasts, as surely as Big Bird is yellow. My sister and her husband will eventually find this out, too, with their little boy and new addition. To help, I've settled on a gift for this new niece or nephew, in lieu of the elusive Book of Lasts. I'm going to send them an item I now believe should be a wardrobe basic for the under-one set: a little crotch-snap T-shirt with the phrase *Carpe Diem*—Seize the Day—puffy-painted across the tummy.

Sue Diaz

Tough Competitions

I sat and cried silently, trying to make sure that my two-year-old did not notice my tears as he played on the floor. I had been ordered on bed rest for pregnancy complications, but finding the order difficult to follow with my whirlwind son, I had decided to let him watch some videos that day about new siblings being born. I hoped that, apart from keeping him stationary for a while, it would also help him understand a little about what it would mean to have a new baby in the family.

Ironically, I had found myself traumatized after watching the videos with him. At first, I didn't know why I was crying, but soon realized that I was feeling guilty for having another baby and having to divide the time, attention, and love that I had been able to give to my first son. And then I started feeling guilty for feeling guilty, because there had been complications and I had dealt with fears of losing the new little life within me. And I wondered to myself, *Will I love my son as much when the new baby comes?*

I wondered for months. I had heard the saying that love is not divided, but multiplied. I didn't know if I believed it. Maybe because I was thinking in terms of tangibles. After all, I thought, *If you have a pie and you have to give it to two people instead of just one, each gets only half the pie, only half of the enjoyment that they would otherwise have gotten from it.* I was the pie, and I feared Hyrum would only enjoy half as much of my love.

As the weeks before the due date slipped away and I was reassured that the baby would make it, a new question began to form in my mind. *Will I be able to love my new daughter as much as I love my son?* She was up for some tough competition. *Would she have his sweet laughter, his spontaneous hugs, his beautiful eyes, his intelligence?* I feared that I might have to keep a lifelong secret from her, the secret that Hyrum had my heart.

The birth was a success, and as I held my bundled daughter and watched her sleeping, my last and latest fear was immediately relieved. I knew that my love for her was brimful. She, too, had my heart, and there were no lifelong secrets to be kept from her.

Grandparents called to notify me that they were bringing Hyrum to the hospital to meet the new baby. A slight amount of unease crept through me as I waited for them, my earliest question surfacing. It was the first time I would see my two little ones together. *Would the scales weigh more in favor of her now, as I saw her next to Hyrum? He was up for some tough competition. Could he hold a candle to her melt-your-heart cry, her softness, her darling nose, and endearing helplessness?*

Twenty minutes later, I heard a knock on the door and greeted my family from the bed as they came in. As Hyrum walked in, we directed him immediately to the baby. He took a look at his little sleeping sister and grinned like Santa had just brought him the gift of his dreams. She was *his* baby. And as I studied his happy face, my heart once again filled with love until it almost spilled out of my eyes in liquid form. And I wondered at how it could happen—how a heart could grow until it had room enough for two.

Tanya Lentz

I Wanted You More

I wanted to be rich
But I wanted you more.
So every time I paid the doctor's bill
I lightly stroked the tiny bulge
That was my priceless treasure,
You.

I wanted to live a life of passion
But I wanted you more.
And since you came to me
I've felt a love I've never known,
Flowing out of me
To you.

I wanted to see the world
But I wanted you more.
So I set aside my traveling
And discovered a world
Right outside my door,
Through your eyes.

I wanted to be carefree
But I wanted you more.
And now I spend my days
Looking at clouds and chasing butterflies
And losing myself
In your laughter.

I wanted so many things
And I got them all,
Because I wanted you.

Barbara Nicks

Organizing Tips

- Avoid perfection at all costs! Being entrenched in motherhood is not the time to let tasks consume you. Doing a "good job" on something that needs completing is good enough! Schedule a time in your calendar to complete a task if necessary. If you don't get to it, then just reschedule it.

- Keep your pediatrician's phone number on the refrigerator door for easy access. And, inside a kitchen cabinet door, consider taping a list of medications, such as Tylenol and Motrin, with the proper dosages for your baby's weight. Some pediatricians' offices have a list ready to go to give to parents.

- Wherever the baby is typically fed, keep the area stocked with snacks, water, a trash can, tissues, magazines, a phone, or whatever else you may want within arm's reach.

8

JOYS OF MOTHERHOOD

Motherhood brings as much joy as ever, but it still brings boredom, exhaustion, and sorrow too. Nothing else will ever make you as happy or as sad, as proud or as tired, for nothing is quite as hard as helping a person develop his own individuality especially while you struggle to keep your own.

Marguerite Kelly and Elia Parson, The Mother's Almanac

There Are Days

Children are the living messages we send to a time we will not see.

John W. Whitehead, *The Stealing of America*, 1983

This morning I sat down on the sofa, coffee in hand, and cried tears of exhaustion . . . there are days like that sometimes. There are days when I wake to the morning sun, after a night when I never really closed my eyes. There are days when the laundry piles up to the ceiling and the dishes tumble out from the sink.

There are days when I long for conversation. Conversation with another adult—*any* adult: a telemarketer, the grocery clerk, or even the grumpy attendant at the Department of Motor Vehicles. There are days when my husband leaves at dawn with a kiss and a wave and returns eight hours later to find me in the same wrinkled T-shirt adorned with new spit-up stains. Sometimes there are days that little handprints and smudgy spaghetti smears decorate the floors and walls, and of course, my pretty white tablecloth. There are days when I wonder how my mother did it, and whether or not I was really cut out for this at all.

But then I think ahead, because I know that there will be a day when I will have time to dig out my gourmet cookbook and make something exotic sounding like "duck l'orange" or "beef Wellington."

There will be a day when I can curl my hair and put on lipstick and eat dinner with my husband at a fancy restaurant whenever we choose. There will be a day when my pearls will come out from hiding, safe from chubby hands clamoring to pull them off their delicate strand, one by one. There will be a day when the mirrors stay clean and the windows are free from fingerprints and splotches and smudges from goodness knows what. There will be a day when I'll have time to learn the tango or the fox-trot, or even take a basket-weaving course if it strikes my fancy.

Ahh, someday there will be a day.

So I trudge on forward to do the laundry and the dishes and calm the tears and clean the stains, and then I stop once more, for there are tears in my eyes again, as I realize something I never really have forgotten. There will be a day when I will pause with a bittersweet smile and look into my husband's eyes.

"Remember those days?" I will ask him as I look around a house so silent and still.

"I do remember," he'll say as he kisses my forehead, "Those were the days."

Emily Weaver

Ode to a Quiet Bathroom

This year I'll turn forty. I'm just waiting for my husband to ask me what I want for my birthday. I've got my answer all prepared. It's probably not what he expects though. In the years before kids, he'd have gotten off easy with jewelry or clothes, dinner out, and a gift certificate to a day spa. But after ten years and three kids, my idea of the perfect birthday gift has evolved. What I want this year is four hours alone and uninterrupted in my own bathroom. Just peace and quiet and porcelain. I suppose that makes me a cheap date but, after ten years of doing whatever I've got to do in the bathroom with an audience, four hours of bathroom solitude sounds better than anything he can charge on his MasterCard or wrap in black "Over the Hill" gift wrap.

My birthday fantasy looks a lot like this: me loitering in the tub with my eyes closed. Around me are no action figures, no stick-on alphabet letters, no naked Barbies. Talk about depressing. The last thing I need, when I'm bent over shaving my legs, is a naked Barbie smirking up at me. I want no little urchins there to offer commentary on my breasts or belly or buttocks or anything else. I don't want to hear that I'm getting fat, but, "Don't worry, Mommy, you look good that way."

I want to shave my legs without delivering a safety lecture about my razor. I don't want to share my shaving cream with anyone no matter how much fun it is. I want to fog up the mirror without having to peak around the curtain and answer, "What letter is this, Mommy? Well, what letter is this?" I want the curtain to stay shut, not be fanned open every few seconds leaving me to explain once again the mechanics of a shower curtain keeping the water *off* the floor. I want the water as hot as I can stand it and not to hear that anyone is taking up all the room. I want *all* the room. I don't once want to hear, "Oops! Guess I forgot to tinkle before I got in the tub." I want to stretch out my legs without it being seen as an invitation for a pony ride. I want to step from the tub without hearing, "Boy, the water goes way down when you get out, Mommy!" and to towel off without having to teach an anatomy lesson entitled, "Why Mommy looks different from Daddy."

And while I'm at it, I want to do what I need to on the toilet without spectators. Not to have to remember who tore off the toilet paper for me the last time so I'm sure everyone gets their turn. I want to pick up a magazine, read an article from start to finish, and actually comprehend what I'm reading. I want to close the door and not have little notes slid underneath with my name on them or tiny fingers wiggling up at me.

Then I want to paint my nails, only mine, no one else's. Not to have the "But, sweetie, nail polish is for girls and mommies, not boys," talk, which is usually followed that evening by the "Oh, honey, I only did his toenails" talk with my husband. I want to give myself a pedicure and a facial, and touch up my roots without once stopping to yell, "I'm in the bathroom. No, I can't come to you. You come to me."

I don't really care where my husband takes the kids. I

Discovering the perpetual fountain of youth.

Advice to Julie

In bringing up children, spend on them half as much money and twice as much time.

Harold S. Hulbert

Looking at my friend, a mom for the first time at thirty-two, is like looking at a portrait of myself ten years ago. There are so many things I want to say to her. There's so much she needs to know. But how can I explain how Jenna's birth will reprioritize her entire life. Things that were life or death to her before won't even enter her mind now. And things that never mattered will become paramount. I want to tell her to let her house go for a while. The cobwebs can wait until her days with an infant are over. She'll never regret a single moment she spends now snuggling, reading, singing, just gazing in amazement at her perfect little gift from God. I want to convince her to graciously accept all the help her friends and family are offering. Let them cook and clean and babysit. The day will come when she can do the same for some of them.

You'll get your old body back, someday, I want to tell her. But your heart will never be yours again. Things like manicures and shoes to match your purse won't seem so important when compared with keeping your baby warm and dry, happy, and fed. I want to tell her how she and her husband will long for some time away only to sit in a restaurant and talk about nothing but the baby, then rush home hours before they're expected because they just can't stand being away from her.

Let's see. Colic drops. Yes! Pull-ups. No! One word about children's music. Raffi! It's music she'll love and you can stand to listen to a million times. Find friends who are in the same boat as you. If you're staying home and tightening your belt, find friends who are, too. They'll be your salvation in those months when you wonder if you can make it or forget why you're home in the first place. If you're going back to work, find friends who are doing the same. You'll need someone to talk with when the doubt and guilt start creeping in. And they will.

But there are so many things I could never put into words. There's the feeling I have when my tiny boy crawls into my lap and whispers, "I marry you, Mama. Do you marry me?" There's the ache in my heart when I watch my ten-year-old Haley already wrestling between whether to be a little girl or a young lady, to see her in her jeans and T-shirt and realize there's a woman's figure trying to emerge underneath. There's the memory of my Molly at two standing on the freshly mopped floor wearing nothing but rubber boots and a smile, holding a clump of ragweed complete with muddy roots and a trail of dirt behind her. It was the sweetest bouquet I ever received.

How can I tell her about the bond between my husband and me, the only person who loves our kids as much as I do? Can I find the words to describe the way it feels to watch my child growing up and realize that not only do I love this half-grown person but I like who she's becoming as well? Can I tell her about the excitement of seeing my children fall in love with books and reading, of watching them struggle with a moral decision, and about the pride of seeing them make the right choice? I guess some things just can't be put into words. But looking at Julie now as she cradles Jenna, all I can think to say is, "It's just gonna keep getting better." I know that in the next few years she'll discover all the joy and wonder I have in this most sacred of callings known as motherhood.

Mimi Greenwood Knight

My Two New Mothers

Grown don't mean nothing to a mother. A child is a child. They get bigger, older, but grown? What's that suppose to mean? In my heart it don't mean a thing.

Toni Morrison, *Beloved,* 1987

It's happened to me and to many of my friends. We became mothers, most of us, many, many years ago. And for every mother I know, there's a story to tell about labor, delivery, adoption, pain, joy, loss, love, and a lifetime of kids growing up.

I did my mom duty. And I loved it.

But, I have to say that nothing has ever been as wondrous as watching the creation of a new mother. My first new mother came into this world in May 1999. I was there at her birth. My son and his wife—recently having moved back from Costa Rica, almost ready to give birth—said to me one day, "Mom, will you be our labor coach?" Wow! No hesitation there. "Of course!" And so I was, a few short weeks later. And by the bedside, I told my daughter-in-law, Kendy, who was busily trying to make this whole thing go away, "Look in my eyes, honey. Keep looking. You'll be okay. I promise!" And she did, and she was.

A few short hours later (it felt like months to her), my granddaughter, Sarah, was born and I was there. As my son wept over his baby daughter, I saw my daughter-in-law and she was new. She was a new mother, my very first new mother. And she was changed forever, and so was I. A daughter, a mother, and a granddaughter all in one moment.

And then it happened again. Six years later at 6:00 AM the phone rang and sure enough it was Sarah. This Sarah is my daughter, after whom her brother's child was named. "Mom, I'm in labor, can you come right now?"

Wow! No hesitation here either. "Sure, honey, I'll be right there." *What was I thinking? Right there?* She lives a thousand miles away, twelve hours by car, no nonstop flights, planes jammed at the February school break. "Wake up, hubby," I called, "Pack my bags, warm the car, I'm going to Virginia. Our baby's having a baby!"

While Ted groggily packed a suitcase, with not necessarily what I would have thought to bring, I jumped on the Internet, found a plane, drove to the airport, made the connecting flight—and there I was in five hours flat, at my daughter's door, before she even went to the hospital.

Twelve long hours later, I welcomed my second granddaughter, Kendy, into the world and met my daughter for the first time as a mother.

It's the little miracles that count most. Kendy looking into my eyes, getting the last seat on the only plane going to Virginia, saying "yes" to those we love without hesitation, and welcoming two new mothers into the world. And two new granddaughters.

Dorothy Firman

My New Job

I got a great new job recently. My responsibilities are varied, so I don't get bored.

I'm my own boss. The job is flexible, although the hours are not. I have the convenience of working from home, and I don't even really need office space. I can be as creative with the position as I want, so the possibilities are endless. The budget isn't very big, but I find I can manage with fairly little. I like not being tied down to a geographical area, because I can take the job wherever I go. Of course, it helps that I have a loyal clientele.

I have one business partner who does the necessary fund-raising during the day. When he's free, he provides coverage for me. We've been in business together for ten years, but we've only been building our client-base for the last three. He's reliable, hardworking, and totally invested. Most important, he's never let me down. I can't think of anyone I'd rather work with, and the clients simply adore him.

A little bit about my clientele: They have only been in this country for less than three years. They're still trying to learn the language, so sometimes communication can be difficult. I know it's extremely frustrating for them, so I try to be patient. They're also trying very hard to learn the culture, and the etiquette and social niceties that will help them better fit into this society of ours. They've got a way to go yet, but their progress has been nothing short of remarkable.

I like to think of myself as tour guide: I show them the sights. I've pretty much single-handedly taught them English. But I'll readily admit for all I've taught them, they've taught me a million things more.

For instance, I teach them the language, but they teach me funny new ways to use it. I teach them the culture, but their questions really make me think about why things are the way they are. I show them a lot of things that they've never seen before, but they've taught me to really look at everything, whether it's a butterfly or the moon, as if I was seeing it for the first time. Most of all, they have taught me about myself—who I am, what I value.

More than anything else the clients are what make this job so worth doing. Not that they're always easy to please. Far from it. They're frequently demanding and irrational. They like things done just so, and want it done on time. Some days, to say the least, this job is a real challenge.

And, I suppose, the only real drawback with this new position is the salary. There isn't one. I work pro bono. I've certainly made more money for doing easier work with fewer responsibilities.

Besides, I definitely don't go totally uncompensated.

When I look into the eyes of my three tiny clients, I see trust. When I look at their young smiles, I see stability. When I watch their eagerness, enthusiasm, joy, and interest, I feel fulfillment because I've been able to help with the installation of all these things. I'll never make big bucks for it, but I'll also never regret the fact that I was able to walk so closely by their sides as they embarked on one of their most important journeys—childhood.

My clients are, quite literally, family to me. And in this business of love and motherhood, that feels just like money in the bank.

Karen C. Driscoll

No Regrets

The moment a child is born, the mother is also born. She never existed before. The woman existed, but the mother, never. A mother is something absolutely new.

Bhagwan Shree Rajneesh

I had a career once. The kind in which you go to an office, work for a specific amount of time, and on designated days, get a paycheck. I did this for years and got pretty good at it. The paychecks increased from time to time as validation of improved skills.

Then I got pregnant. My career wardrobe became obsolete. I relied on a really comfortable, stretchy pair of knit pants that I wore a lot. I took lots of bathroom breaks and found myself eating far more lunch than any of my coworkers. Once I spent an entire afternoon napping in the employee sickroom.

But still, I went to the office each morning, remained there for an agreed amount of time, and got paid for it.

Then I gave birth. I told the office in advance that I was resigning because I was to be a stay-at-home mom. My supervisor, an extravagantly ambitious woman with fabulous career suits and a French manicure, couldn't believe what I told her. She had assumed I would take maternity leave and then return—tired, baggy, even occasionally leaking, but determined to pick up where I left off. As I hoisted my nine-month girth from the deep leather couch in her office (which itself would have made a pretty nice napping location), I said no, I wasn't coming back.

In fact, it took most of a year before I could imagine ever doing anything but nursing the baby. In my postpartum derangement, I thought I was to spend the entire rest of my life with my shirt open, stupidly gazing at reruns on the television that my husband put in a corner of the living room to keep me engaged in a facsimile of real life.

Finally, one day I called someone who might hire me to work from home. And he did. With the baby finally on a sleep schedule, I had nap times available to work. It didn't matter that I hadn't showered, or that there were spit-up stains on my shoulder. Nobody saw me.

Now from time to time I get a check in the mail. I am a (barely) working mom. Still, this life is different than the career I once pursued.

Once, work breaks consisted of loitering by the coffeemaker, talking over whatever was on television last night, or complaining with my coworkers about the job. Now, work breaks consist of folding laundry or unloading the dishwasher. I have only the dog with whom to discuss things and nobody hears my complaints.

"Casual Fridays" used to mean relaxed clothes at work and long lunches with my colleagues. Now every day is as casual as every other, and a lunch out is likely to mean trying to eat a bagged picnic at the park with a toddler who won't sit still.

I once used my commute to sing at the top of my lungs with the radio. It's a real stress reducer. Now my commute

Be Careful What You Wish For

Be careful what you wish for. You just might get it. As my two-year-old sits astride the potty grinning from ear to ear over his first "success," I can feel a lump growing in my throat. This is what I wanted, right? For my youngest child to be potty-wise? No more diapers. No more paying those diaper prices. No more making sure I have an ample supply before leaving the house. No more feeling guilty because I opted for the convenience of disposable over the environmentally responsible cloth ones. No more clipping diaper coupons, which I never remembered to use. This is the day I've been dreaming about? Isn't it?

But with the end of the diaper era, I see the beginning of the end of a most meaningful chapter of my life. My mind flashes back to the insecure, nervous parent I was, just seven years ago, when I brought Haley home from the hospital. I remember smiling at the nurses as David wheeled me out of the New Family Center while inside I was screaming *Are you people crazy? I don't know how to take care of this baby!* I think about the sleepless nights I spent, not because Haley kept me awake, but because I had to jump up every few minutes to make sure she was still breathing.

· I remember the overwrought, inept mother I was when just twenty months later, I brought little Molly home and attempted to balance myself between a demanding toddler and a premature newborn, while trying to figure out how my marriage figured into all of this, not to mention any chance for a life of my own.

Next came three years of wrestling over whether to have a third, ending with a very pleasant surprise—the birth of my perfect baby boy. The day we brought Hewson home from the hospital, the five of us spent the morning on the bed just snuggling and falling in love with each other. *This is a family!* I thought. *I feel sorry for anyone who's not a part of it.*

Has so much time passed since that day? When did my baby get this big? With Haley and Molly I tried to speed along each phase of their baby and toddlerhood. "I wonder if she'll be sitting by Christmas?" "I hope she's walking by summer." I pushed them into learning their colors, their numbers, their alphabet. Now, I wish I could slam on the breaks. I just want to drop to my knees right here on the bathroom floor and beg him to let me put him back in a diaper, a little gingham romper, and high-top shoes. Maybe we'll tackle the potty next year.

To think of all the times over the past seven years when I've longed for a life of my own, to have time to pamper myself, to read like I used to, to have an uninterrupted phone conversation or bath. Suddenly all of that seems superfluous when compared with the feeling of knowing exactly who I am. I am this mom, wife, writer, teacher, storyteller, gardener, baker, volunteer person. I've loved that feeling of knowing beyond a shadow of a doubt that I'm in the right place at the right time. Whenever I feel overwhelmed with things I'm not getting done, I can stop, read a book with one of my children, and know, beyond a shadow of a doubt, that there's nothing more important, more monumental, more future-building than what I am doing at that moment.

I wonder who I'll be when all of that's taken from me. I wonder how I'll pass my days when I finally have the freedom for which I've longed. What will it be like to crawl into bed without first tucking three warm, little bodies under their own covers? How will I spend my mornings when I'm not drinking my coffee with the expectation of sleepy little feet shuffling my way for that first morning hug?

I close my eyes and make a pledge not to take any of it for granted, to enjoy every hectic, exhausting, demanding moment I have left in this chapter of my life. I pledge not to take a single snuggle or fish kiss or phonetically spelled love note for granted. Hewson is staring up at me. I know it's time to lift him off the potty and run to the phone to tell his dad the "good news." I wonder what his reaction will be.

Mimi Greenwood Knight

True Confession

Mother's arms are made of tenderness, and
sweet sleep blesses the child who lies therein.

Victor Hugo

I have a true confession to make: I liked nursing my twins.

For years I would have said that I liked nursing because it saved money—money I spent on a cleaning service every other week. I would have explained that the time others spent warming bottles in the dark of the night, I passed reclining while feeding my babies.

My discussion would have included how nursing gave me a chance to sit while that extra pregnancy weight flowed out of me. Or maybe how sweating with two little heaters attached to my chest took off the weight. I would tell about consuming large amounts of food and still returning to my pre-pregnancy size.

It didn't take long for me to choose breast-feeding over bottle-feeding my multiple infants. After researching the methods, I picked the one that required fewer housekeeping skills. My years of stacking dirty plates suggested I was unprepared to tackle more dishes, especially sterile ones.

A new U-shaped nursing pillow rode along when my husband and I left for the hospital early one June morning. Later in the day, I whipped that pillow out as the nurse brought me our two babes to feed. We all began to learn together. Pictures show me, a mother for only a few hours, clutching two tiny bundles like footballs. A former flag football player, I had played defense because I couldn't always keep the football in my hands. Now I could carry two "footballs" that wriggled and squirmed.

Learning to feed two took time, especially since my milk also took its time coming in. Politeness flew out the door, even with my parents in our house for three weeks. Their daughter had become an island girl, sitting around topless every three hours. Nursing shirts didn't seem to work with two babies—unless one baby liked taking its milk with a mouthful of cotton. I didn't know to worry when my milk didn't gush in until the kids' fourth night in this world. Despite my inexperience, the babies stayed healthy. The morning after the taps began to flow, I rushed to buy breast pads—a fashion accessory that became this girl's best friend.

Within weeks I became comfortable nursing almost anywhere. I learned to nurse two in public without exposing the faucets that sprang into action with the slightest cries from my babies, or from stray cats. I, a past member of the IBT Committee in my sorority (hint: the first letter stands for "Itty"), fed two infants at once, just as God had created my body to do.

I spent those early no-free-hands months topless in our basement, watching reruns. Often as I sat frozen in place, my dog would join me on the couch. Her head on the edge of the pillow, she would look at me as if to say, "You're just sitting there. Sure, you can pet me." As if I had a third hand.

When I hit the look-no-hands period, I thought I had died and gone to heaven. Leaving the television off, I read voraciously, wrote thank-you notes, ate, drank, and talked on the phone. I didn't understand why my friend, her younger child already three and a half, momentarily couldn't talk when she heard little baby suckling noises.

In my fatigue, I began to fall asleep during nighttime feedings. One night my son feasted from 1:00 AM to 4:00 AM while I snoozed. My right side looked like it did when I was eleven, while the left side looked like something out of *Playboy*. Luckily, we were almost finished with middle-of-the-night feedings when the incident occurred. As if he knew it was last call for after-hours drinks.

Tandem nursing allowed the kids to explore whatever was nursing next to them. The first time I saw them holding hands I almost cried. Later they began to poke eyes and pull hair—after that they only nursed together first thing in the morning, the time of serious eating. Their final public tandem nursing act occurred on New Year's Eve, more than six months after their first performances. They looked like a Punch and Judy show under their cover cloth. I could tell that nursing in the new year would be different. I didn't want my body to participate in anything that resembled their pacifier-stealing games.

The babies continued to nurse until right before their first birthday. I weaned them to one feeding a day, but spent six weeks letting go of the final nursing time. My mother-in-law said she'd buy the formula if I wanted to stop completely. I didn't answer her—she had never felt the little hands fluttering on her ribs.

Oh, the indignities I experienced. Showers coincided with milk baths, courtesy of a good letdown reflex. Whenever my husband spied my temporary hourglass figure, he heard, "You touch them and you die." I made love with a bra on (did we really have sex?). In the early morning light, I often rolled over so the waterbed's warmth soothed my throbbing breasts while the children learned to sleep through the night. Once in Jazzercise, I reached high and left a breast pad on the floor.

My chest aches as I remember those days. Oh no, it wasn't the money, weight loss, or ease that mattered. As a mother who received two babies at once, I rarely got to sit and hold our little creations. Mandatory feedings became time to bond and get to know each other. Although my heart rate climbed high getting screaming infants ready to eat, it slowed as the life force flowed from me into them. Sometimes when we finished, we three would just sit there, unwilling to move.

My husband cooked numerous meals and changed seemingly endless numbers of diapers so I could maintain my strength. His loving actions helped give our kids an opportunity to be breast-fed, but they also gave me the chance to do one of the things I enjoyed most about early motherhood.

I liked nursing.

Trina Lambert

Occupation: Mom

Being a full-time mother is one of the highest salaried jobs. . . . since the payment is pure love.
Mildred B. Vermont

If you had asked me what I wanted to be growing up, I could have rattled off at least a dozen possible careers, including author, editor, counselor, and teacher. There was no doubt in my mind that I would one day go to college and be a professional of some sort. I even fantasized about being grown-up, breezing down the streets of a bustling city in my high heels and pantsuit, carrying a stylish briefcase, and looking important. I envisioned my office on the tenth floor of a building, where I would be surrounded by perky, businesslike people who would praise me for my hard work and creative ideas and bring me freshly brewed coffee. Of course, to top it off, I would bring home a substantial paycheck, which I would split evenly between my savings account and lavish purchases. In this fantasy, there were no dirty feet pattering around the floors, no milk-stained suits, and no 3:00 AM feedings.

This fantasy, as nice as it was, was rudely interrupted

by an eight-pound little being who came into the world on a sunny July day and changed my life forever. He spent the first three months of his life crying incessantly, despite every effort under the sun to keep him content. My Friday nights were suddenly consumed by feeding and burping sessions that took place in a rocking chair with country music television blaring in the background. And that pantsuit I had in mind? Try a stretched-out, spit-up-stained terry cloth jogging suit that became my staple uniform during those exhausting blurs of days and nights. Forty pounds and a few stretch marks later, I had become *Mom*.

Three months into this exhausting stretch of motherhood, I made a frantic dash to the library in search of some sort of manual that would explain just how these babies worked. If this was my "job," I was bound and determined to do it right, despite the fact that a promotion or a raise wasn't looking too promising anytime soon. I was inundated by dozens of books on burping, changing, loving, singing to, talking to, and playing with baby. Of course, there were the books on how to get baby to sleep, which I was certain were written by some male who could not possibly have had children, or at least ones that cried. And then there were the generic "Your Baby" books, showing a happy, smiling mother in a nicely pressed silk shirt and lipstick gazing down at her cherub adoringly. After much thought, I came home empty-handed, convinced that I was indeed the only mother on the face of the planet who didn't know how to do her "job."

Frustrated by my apparent lack of mothering skills, I dove back into my college classes, determined to get one step closer to that pantsuit, high-rise building, and nifty paycheck. When my peers asked me what I planned to do for a living, I spouted off the usual possibilities, all the while intently aware that I was sporting a large spit-up stain on my shoulder and carrying around my school books in an overloaded nylon diaper bag. Everything about me, from the leftover baby pouch to the bags under the eyes screamed *Mom*, yet I was still not sure I was quite equipped for that job.

And then came another day that changed my life. I accidentally slipped into a mother-baby class, thinking it was my world history class, and was amazed to see mothers and babies of all shapes and sizes crawling around on the floor, clapping their hands, and singing happy songs. As their laughter filled the air, I clutched my diaper bag/backpack and wondered if I too might be able to join in the fun.

As it turned out, mother-baby class was far more interesting than world history. There were renditions of *Row, Row, Row Your Boat* to be memorized, colorful puzzles to be put together, and of course, lots of "my horrible labor" stories to be swapped. As the weeks went by, I learned to stop hiding by the diaper bag cubbies and made my way into the center of the room, where other spit-up-stained mommies were waiting with sympathetic ears and open arms. Our conversations of "Little Constipated Johnny," "Diaper Rash Suzy," and "Sleep Not Nellie" became the common buzz in the room. I met all sorts of women, from an all-natural who ground her own baby food to a gal who had just left her corporate job with all its perks to stay home with her premature daughter. Suddenly, I was surrounded by a sea of nodding heads, offering me baby wipes and good advice, and I was not alone.

Four children later, I'm proud to say that I'm still employed as a *mom*. Oh sure, I have lots of days where I'd give my right arm to wake up, hop into a pair of nylons and heels, and dash out the door to my high-rise job. But right now, I'm keeping pretty busy playing taxi driver, chef, nurse, counselor, and housekeeper. There are lunches to be made, bottoms to be wiped, and doctor trips galore. There are stories to be read, kisses to be dished out, and owies to be mended. As all mothers know, a mother's job never ends.

The other night, as I slipped into bed after stepping on a clump of Cheerios that had become imbedded in my carpet, I couldn't help but chuckle. I certainly didn't set out to find this "job." Had there been an interview, I'm pretty sure I would have flunked it. And had I known how hard it would be and how little training would be provided, I'm pretty sure I would have said "no thanks." But I'm sure glad I signed up. I wouldn't trade all those messy, milky kisses for all the pantsuits and free coffee in the world!

Karen Koczwara

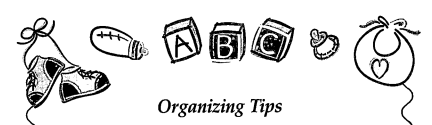

Organizing Tips

• Keep a large box with your baby's name on it for keepsakes that you gather the first year. Include items such as the ID bracelet from the hospital and a copy of the birth announcement.

•Before you know it, you may have piles of photos of your children lying around. Purchasing photo boxes with labeled sections can help organize your pictures until you're ready to put them in photo albums.

• As your children get older, organize your thoughts and goals on a greater scale. Before you know it, you will have the time to conquer aspirations in addition to motherhood that you once thought to be impossible.

More Chicken Soup?

Many of the stories and poems you have read in this book were submitted by readers like you who had read earlier Chicken Soup for the Soul books. We publish many Chicken Soup for the Soul books every year. We invite you to contribute a story to one of these future volumes.

Stories may be up to twelve hundred words and must uplift or inspire. You may submit an original piece, something you have read, or your favorite quotation on your refrigerator door.

To obtain a copy of our submission guidelines and a listing of upcoming Chicken Soup books, please write, fax, or check one of our websites.

Please send your submissions to:

Chicken Soup for the Soul
Website: www.chickensoup.com
P.O. Box 30880
Santa Barbara, CA 93130
fax: 805-563-2945

We will be sure that both you and the author are credited for your submission.

For information about speaking engagements, other books, audiotapes, workshops, and training programs, please contact any of our authors directly.

Supporting Others

In the spirit of supporting others, the publisher and coauthors of *Chicken Soup for the New Mom's Soul* will donate a portion of the proceeds of this book to the **Y- ME National Breast Cancer Organization.**™

The Y-ME National Breast Cancer Organization (Y-ME) is a Chicago-based national nonprofit organization with the mission to ensure—through information, empowerment, and peer support—that no one faces breast cancer alone. Y-ME does not raise money for research. We're here today for those who can't wait for tomorrow's cure.

At the center of the organization is the Y-ME National Breast Cancer Hotline, the only 24/7 call center operated by trained peer counselors who are breast cancer survivors. They take more than 40,000 calls a year. Y-ME counselors do not give medical advice but give emotional support and information about breast cancer, medical procedures, and treatment options. Hotline calls are interpreted in 150 languages.

The organization was founded over a kitchen table in 1978 by the late Ann Marcou and Mimi Kaplan, two breast cancer patients who sought to provide support for fellow breast cancer patients and their loved ones. From these humble beginnings, Y-ME transformed into a national organization that helped revolutionize the way breast cancer patients access information and make decisions about their health care. Nearly thirty years later, Y-ME is a premier resource for breast cancer information and services, all provided completely free of charge.

Y-ME's newsletters, publications, brochures, and website (at www.y-me.org) provide information and support in Spanish and English to those touched by breast cancer. Other Y-ME programs include: Match Programs for patients who have similar diagnoses and life experiences, and for husbands and partners of women with breast cancer; the Wig & Prosthesis Bank for those with limited resources; the monthly ShareRing Network Teleconference; and *A Day for You* and *Friends of Ann & Mimi*—programs for the medically underserved.

Y-ME's advocacy program works to increase breast cancer research funding, support breast cancer–related clinical studies, and ensure quality health care for all.

The organization has affiliates throughout the nation that provide services such as support groups, early detection and teen workshops, wigs and prostheses for women with limited resources, and advocacy on breast cancer-related policies in their communities.

Each year on Mother's Day, the organization holds the Y-ME Race to Empower in Chicago and Y-ME Walk to Empower events across the country. In 2006, nearly 40,000 people took part, raising a total of $6 million in Chicago, Denver, Houston, Miami, Sacramento, San Diego, Seattle, Tulsa, and Washington, D.C. Eighty percent of each dollar raised benefits programs and services offered free of charge to those seeking information and support when facing breast cancer. Y-ME is further expanding its Mother's Day tradition by adding Walk to Empower events in Atlanta, Cleveland, and Phoenix in 2007.

Charity Navigator, an independent evaluator of nonprofits, gives Y-ME its highest rating of four stars for sound fiscal management. Y-ME meets all of the National Health Council's forty-one standards of excellence—best practices that encompass the areas of governance, personnel policies, programs' financing, fund raising, accounting and reporting, and evaluation.

If you or someone you know needs breast cancer information or support, call the 24-hour Y-ME National Breast Cancer Hotline at 1-800-221-2141 or 1-800-986-9505 (Spanish).

Who Is Jack Canfield?

Jack Canfield is the cocreator and editor of the Chicken Soup for the Soul series, which *Time* magazine has called "the publishing phenomenon of the decade." The series now has 105 titles with over 100 million copies in print in forty-one languages. Jack is also the coauthor of eight other bestselling books including *The Success Principles: How to Get from Where You Are to Where You Want to Be, Dare to Win, The Aladdin Factor, You've Got to Read This Book,* and *The Power of Focus: How to Hit Your Business and Personal and Financial Targets with Absolute Certainty.*

Jack has recently developed a telephone coaching program and an online coaching program based on his most recent book *The Success Principles.* He also offers a seven-day Breakthrough to Success seminar every summer, which attracts 400 people from fifteen countries around the world.

Jack has conducted intensive personal and professional development seminars on the principles of success for over 900,000 people in twenty-one countries around the world. He has spoken to hundreds of thousands of others at numerous conferences and conventions and has been seen by millions of viewers on national television shows such as *The Today Show, Fox and Friends, Inside Edition, Hard Copy,* CNN's *Talk Back Live, 20/20, Eye to Eye,* the *NBC Nightly News,* and the *CBS Evening News.*

Jack is the recipient of many awards and honors, including three honorary doctorates and a Guinness World Records Certificate for having seven books from the Chicken Soup for the Soul series appearing on the *New York Times* bestseller list on May 24, 1998.

To write to Jack or for inquiries about Jack as a speaker, his coaching programs, or his seminars, use the following contact information:

The Canfield Companies
P.O. Box 30880 • Santa Barbara, CA 93130
phone: 805-563-2935 • fax: 805-563-2945
E-mail: info@jackcanfield.com or
visit his website at www.jackcanfield.com

Who Is Mark Victor Hansen?

In the area of human potential, no one is more respected than Mark Victor Hansen. For more than thirty years, Mark has focused solely on helping people from all walks of life reshape their personal vision of what's possible. His powerful messages of possibility, opportunity, and action have created powerful change in thousands of organizations and millions of individuals worldwide.

He is a sought-after keynote speaker, bestselling author, and marketing maven. Mark's credentials include a lifetime of entrepreneurial success and an extensive academic background. He is a prolific writer with many bestselling books, such as *The One Minute Millionaire, Cracking the Millionaire Code, How to Make the Rest of Your Life the Best of Your Life, The Power of Focus, The Aladdin Factor,* and *Dare to Win,* in addition to the Chicken Soup for the Soul series. Mark has made a profound influence through his library of audios, videos, and articles in the areas of big thinking, sales achievement, wealth building, publishing success, and personal and professional development.

Mark is the founder of the MEGA Seminar Series. MEGA Book Marketing University and Building Your MEGA Speaking Empire are annual conferences where Mark coaches and teaches new and aspiring authors, speakers, and experts on building lucrative publishing and speaking careers. Other MEGA events include MEGA Info-Marketing and My MEGA Life.

As a philanthropist and humanitarian, Mark works tirelessly for organizations such as Habitat for Humanity, American Red Cross, March of Dimes, Childhelp USA, and many others. He is the recipient of numerous awards that honor his entrepreneurial spirit, philanthropic heart, and business acumen. He is a lifetime member of the Horatio Alger Association of Distinguished Americans, an organization that honored Mark with the prestigious Horatio Alger Award for his extraordinary life achievements.

Mark Victor Hansen is an enthusiastic crusader of what's possible and is driven to make the world a better place.

Mark Victor Hansen & Associates, Inc.
P.O. Box 7665 • Newport Beach, CA 92658
phone: 949-764-2640 • fax: 949-722-6912
www.markvictorhansen.com

Who Is Patty Aubery?

As the president of Chicken Soup for the Soul Enterprises and a #1 *New York Times* bestselling coauthor, Patty Aubery knows what it's like to juggle work, family, and social obligations—along with the responsibility of developing and marketing the more than 80 million Chicken Soup books and licensed goods worldwide.

She knows because she's been with Jack Canfield's organization since the early days—before Chicken Soup took the country by storm. Jack was still telling these heartwarming stories then, in his training programs, workshops, and keynote presentations, and it was Patty who directed the labor of love that went into compiling and editing the original 101 Chicken Soup stories. Later, she supported the daunting marketing effort and steadfast optimism required to bring it to millions of readers worldwide.

Today, Patty is the mother of two active boys—J.T. and Chandler—exemplifying that special combination of commitment, organization, and life balance all working women want to have. She's been known to finish at the gym by 6:00 AM, guest-host a radio show at 6:30, catch a flight by 9:00 to close a deal—and be back in time for soccer with the kids. But perhaps the most notable accolade for this special working woman is the admiration and love her friends, family, staff, and peers hold for her.

Of her part in the Chicken Soup family, Patty says, "I'm always encouraged, amazed, and humbled by the storytellers I meet when working on any Chicken Soup book, but by far the most poignant have been those stories of women in the working world, overcoming incredible odds and—in the face of all challenges—excelling as only women could do."

Patty is also the coauthor of several other bestselling titles: *Chicken Soup for the Christian Soul, Christian Family Soul,* and *Christian Woman's Soul, Chicken Soup for the Expectant Mother's Soul, Chicken Soup for the Sister's Soul, Chicken Soup for the Sister's Soul 2,* and *Chicken Soup for the Surviving Soul.*

She is married to a successful international entrepreneur, Jeff Aubery, and together with J. T. and Chandler, they make their home in Santa Barbara, California. Patty can be reached at:

Self-Esteem Seminars
P.O. Box 30880
Santa Barbara, CA 93130
Phone: 805-563-2935 • Fax: 805-563-2945

Contributors

Several of the stories in this book were taken from previously published sources, such as books, magazines, and newspapers. These sources are acknowledged in the permissions section. If you would like to contact any of the contributors for information about their writing or would like to invite them to speak in your community, look for their contact information included in their biographies.

The remainder of the stories were submitted by readers of our previous Chicken Soup for the Soul books who responded to our requests for stories. We have also included information about them.

Susanna Hickman Bartee is a military wife and freelance writer living in Missouri with her husband and five children and can be reached at bartees7@earthlink.net.

Heather Best fell in love with writing at the age of thirteen when she won her first poetry contest. She is very involved in the youth ministry at her church in Malvern, Arkansas, and loves sharing her life with her husband, Nic, and their two beautiful toddlers, Justus and Evan.

SG Birch received her bachelor of arts degree from Bishop's University. She went on to study natural nutrition while at home with her two small children and is now a practicing registered holistic nutritionist, home-office mom, and nutrition writer. You can contact her at shannon@holisticnutrition.ca.

Heather Black is a writer living in Gainesville, Florida. Her story originally appeared in *Woman's World* magazine.

Paula F. Blevins and her husband, David, live in Gallipolis, Ohio, with three wonderful kids and several pets that seem to keep multiplying. She is the author of the For Hymn Mystery Series and enjoys writing for children as well as adults. Contact Paula through her website at http://www.paulafblevins.com.

Douglas M. Brown has been writing since the sixth grade. He has been published in religious magazines and *Chicken Soup for the Latter-day Saint's Soul*. He and his wife, JuVene, live in West Jordan, Utah, and have seven children. You may contact Doug at d8snraysons@yahoo.com.

Stephanie Ray Brown of Henderson, Kentucky, has been happily married to her Webster County High School sweetheart for twenty years. She continues to adore him after all these years, especially when she looks at their daughter, Savannah, who has her daddy's big brown eyes, and their son, Cameron, who has his dad's perfect chin.

Kevin Butler is a stay-at-home dad and student of Murray State University's creative writing program. He enjoys writing short stories of all genres and spending time with his beautiful wife and daughter. E-mail him at kevin32080@yahoo.com.

Martha Campbell is a graduate of Washington University, St. Louis School of Fine Arts, and a former writer/designer for Hallmark Cards. She has been a freelance cartoonist and book illustrator since 1973. She can be reached at P.O. Box 2538, Harrison, AR or at marthaf@alltel.net.

April Smith Carpenter, from Mississippi, is a wife and a proud mother of two. She received a bachelor of arts from Lambuth University and a master of arts in religion from Memphis Theological Seminary. She enjoys traveling, writing, football, and aerobics.

Robin Clifton lives in New Hope, Minnesota, with her husband, Jerry, and their four children. She grew up in the Minnesota river town of Red Wing, where her story takes place. The proud grandparents (her parents), Bob and Genere Gordish, still live there today.

Lynn Dean is a Colorado writer and mother of three. She has published over 500 articles in more than 100 publications in over thirty-five states and several countries. Lynn specializes in the areas of parenting, health, lifestyle, and women's issues. Please visit Lynn's website at www.lynnmdean.com.

Sue Diaz is an essayist, author, and writing teacher whose work has appeared in numerous regional and national publications, including *Newsweek, Family Circle, Christian Science Monitor, Woman's Day,* and *Reader's Digest*. She is also a frequent on-air essayist on National Public Radio. Her website, www.suediaz.com, tells all.

Karen C. Driscoll lives with her husband and their four children in Connecticut.

Lisa Duffy-Korpics is a freelance writer and social studies teacher in Montgomery, New York. Her work has appeared in several Chicken Soup for the Soul books. She lives with her husband, Jason, ten-year-old daughter, Emmaleigh, and thirteen-year-old son, Charles . . . who no longer wears baby shoes!

Martine Ehrenclou received her master's degree in psychology with honors from Pepperdine University in 2003. She is a copywriter for creative professionals and is working on a nonfiction healthcare book and a novel. She teaches writing classes to teenage girls at a rehab center near Los Angeles. E-mail Martine at Ehrenclou@aol.com.

Nancy Engler lives in Arizona with her husband, two daughters, and two dogs. She enjoys writing children's literature and her stories and poems have been published in a variety of places including *Wee Ones, Boy's Quest,* and *Story Friends*. In her spare time, Nancy loves to read, paint, and draw.

Dorothy Firman is a coauthor of *Chicken Soup for the Mother and Daughter Soul* and the forthcoming *Chicken Soup for the Soul: Celebrating Mothers and Daughters*. She is also the coauthor of *Daughters and Mothers: Making It Work*. A speaker, workshop leader, and psychotherapist, Dorothy can be reached at dfirman@comcast.net.

Peggy Frezon is a freelance writer from New York. She is a frequent contributor to *Guideposts, Sweet 16, Positive Thinking,* and *Angels on Earth*. Her work has also appeared in *Teaching Tolerance, Soul Matters,* and various Chicken Soup for the Soul books. Contact Peggy through her website at http://peggyfrezon.googlepages.com.

Sally Friedman is the proud mother of three adult daughters who taught her many of life's lessons. She has been a freelance writer for three decades, with work published in the *New York Times, Ladies Home Journal, Family Circle,* and *Home,* along with newspapers around the country. E-mail her at pinegander@aol.com.

Jonny Hawkins dedicates his "fountain of youth" cartoon in this book to his precious baby girl who awaits in the womb and to her mother, his wife, Carissa, who is going to be a new mom . . . again. His cartoons have appeared in hundreds of publications and in annual cartoon-a-day calendars and books. He can be reached at jonnyhawkins2nz@yahoo.com.

Cindy Hval and her husband, Derek, are raising four sons, ages six through sixteen, in Spokane, Washington. Her work has appeared in *Chicken Soup for the Mother and Son Soul* and in *Northwest Woman* and *ByLine* magazines. She's currently a correspondent for the *Spokesman Review* newspaper. Contact her at dchval@juno.com.

Eva Juliuson eventually remarried after her first husband Steve's death. She and her husband, Dwight, share seven children and seven grandchildren. Besides sharing her passion for God through writing, Eva sends out short, regular e-mail prayers to encourage others in a deeper prayer life. To receive them, contact her at evajuliuson@hotmail.com.

Elizabeth Kann is a doctor who lives in Pennsylvania with her husband and two children. Her essays have appeared in the *Pittsburgh Post-Gazette, SHE Caribbean, Chocolate for the Soul Volume II,* and elsewhere. She and her sister coauthored the children's picture book, *Pinkalicious* (HarperCollins 2006). Visit her online at www.elizabethkann.com.

Susan A. Karas is a freelance writer who has been published in *Guideposts, Sweet 16,* and *Positive Thinking* magazines, among others. Her proudest achievement to date is winning a coveted spot in a national writing contest. When she is not writing, Susan enjoys reading and gardening. Contact her at MsSusanKaras@yahoo.com.

Julie Bloss Kelsey is a freelance writer and stay-at-home mom. She enjoys writing magazine articles and stories for children. Her work has appeared in *Washington Parent* and *Natural Family Online.* Julie lives in Maryland with her husband, John, and their two young boys. You can reach her at julie.kelsey@alumni.duke.edu.

Mary Knight is an inspirational writer, speaker, and workshop facilitator. "First Night Home" is excerpted from "Love Letters Before Birth and Beyond," a mother's journal for pregnant and new moms. Her son, Zach, is now twenty-seven years old, 6' 2", and a cellist! For more about Mary and her book, visit mothersjournal.com or e-mail her at singleye@whidbey.com.

Mimi Greenwood Knight is a freelance writer and mother of four living in what's left of South Louisana. Her work has appeared in *Parents Magazine, American Baby, Working Mother, Christian Parenting Today,* and others. She's especially proud to have her essays appear in several Chicken Soup for the Soul books.

Karen Koczwara received her bachelor of arts in English literature from Chico State University in 2000. She currently lives in Arizona with her husband and four children, ages one through ten. When she is not changing diapers or chauffering children to soccer games, Karen enjoys writing, playing piano, cooking, and scrapbooking.

Tom Krause is an international motivational speaker specializing in educational audiences and parent groups. He lives in Nixa, Missouri, with wife, Amy, and two redheaded boys, Tyler and Sam.

Trina Lambert is a Colorado-based writer, volunteer, and at-home mom. She lives with her husband, daughter, and son. Although she misses the days of nursing, Trina is knee-deep in homework, car pools, and other activities. True confession: her kids are in high school now! Find out more about Trina at www.trinalambert.com.

Kathryn Lay is a full-time writer living in Texas with her family. She writes for magazines and anthologies and is the author of a children's novel, *Crown Me!* and a soon-to-be-published picture book, *Josh's Magic Pumpkin*. Check out her website at www.kathrynlay.com or e-mail her at rlay15@aol.com.

Ginger LeBlanc works in public relations and lives with her husband, her son, and her feisty wiener dog in Baton Rouge, Louisiana. She can be reached via e-mail at lovemydox@gmail.com.

Tanya Lentz is a wife and a mother of three. She received her bachelor of science in marriage, family, and human development from Brigham Young University in 2001. She is passionate about writing, nature, and family. Her story "Meeting Jeanie" appears in *Chicken Soup for the Mother of Preschooler's Soul*.

Shannon Dunn Lowe lives in Oklahoma with her husband, Mac, and her four children. Between PTA meetings and loads of laundry, she writes a daily faith and parenting blog at www.rocksinmydryer.typepad.com.

Catherine Madera is a contributing writer for *Guideposts* magazine. Her stories, both ghosted and personal, have appeared in *Guideposts, Positive Thinking*, and various anthologies. She also enjoys writing for equine publications and is an avid horseback rider. Catherine lives with her husband and two children in the Pacific Northwest. Contact her at www.catherinemadera.com.

Stephanie McCarty writes the column, *Fumbling Toward Motherhood*, which appears regularly in print and online publications. She worked in public affairs for more than a decade before launching her writing career. Please contact her at Stephanie@fumblingtowardmotherhood.com or visit www.fumblingtoward motherhood.com to read more of her work.

Dahlynn McKowen is a loving wife, dedicated mother of two, and full-time author. An active coauthor for Chicken Soup for the Soul books, Dahlynn has created many new titles, including *Fisherman's Soul, Entrepreneur's Soul*, and the upcoming *Soul in Menopause, Red Hat Society Soul*, and *Sisters' and Brothers' Soul*. Contact her at www.PublishingSyndicate.com.

Carol Sjostrom Miller and her husband, Jack, live in New Jersey with their daughters, Stephanie and Lauren. Her articles, essays, and humor pieces—written while her family sleeps—have appeared in *Parents, Parenting, Family Fun, The Christian Science Monitor*, and *Chicken Soup for the Mother and Daughter Soul*. She can be reached at miller.carol@yahoo.com.

Stephanie Mirmina is an elementary school reading specialist. She lives in Arlington, Virginia. She loves traveling, reading, cooking, and hanging out with her husband and new son.

Lava Mueller spent much of her early years of motherhod on the phone with Adriana Elliot, generating raw material for their play, *Mommy Talk*, a comedy in three acts about motherhood, sexuality, and anger. Lava lives in southern Vermont with her husband, Andy, and her children, Sophie and Max. Contact her at limeyfoe@sover.net

Barbara Nicks began writing poems soon after the birth of her first child, who is now one of her sixth-grade students in east Texas. She enjoys reading, scrapbooking, and traveling with her family. She can be contacted at bnicks@email.com.

Linda O'Connell has been published in *Chicken Soup for the Gardener's Soul*, several literary and mainstream magazines, newspapers, and online journals. She leads a senior citizen writers' group and has been an early childhood educator for thirty years. Linda enjoys camping with her husband. Contact her at billin7@juno.com.

Mark Parisi's "off the mark" comic panel has been syndicated since 1987 and is distributed by United Media. Mark's humor also graces greeting cards, T-shirts, calendars, magazines, newsletters, and books. Please vist his website at www.offthemark.com. Lynn is his wife/business partner, and their daughter, Jen, contributes with inspiration (as do three cats).

Kathleen Partak lives in northern California with her husband, Dave, and their young son, Mason. Besides penning a weekly e-mail column for the past seven years, Kathleen also writes for local publications on topics including real estate mortgages, today's technology, and military life (Dave is a National Guard member). She can be reached at kdpartak@yahoo.com.

Maggie Wolff Peterson has been a professional writer for twenty-five years, with pieces published nationally, regionally, and locally. She lives in Virginia with her husband, son, and dog.

Becky Povich began pursuing her writing career when she was in her forties. She wrote about her family, both past and present, in a local newspaper. She is working on publishing a book of her stories in 2007. Please e-mail her at beapov@aol.com.

Joe Rector is a high school English teacher and a freelance columnist. He writes for three newspapers in Knoxville and has written feature stories for *Sweets* magazine. Future endeavors include finding a publisher for his book of columns and starting a new magazine for teachers. Contact him at joerector@comcast.net.

Sallie Rodman is a freelance writer living in Los Alamitos, California. She has contributed to numerous Chicken Soup anthologies, various magazines, and the *Orange County Register*. Sallie enjoys inspirational writing, reading, and writing, and family barbecues, especially when all her children and grandchildren can get together at one time. E-mail her at sa.rodman@verizon.net.

Dan Rosandich has published cartoons for thirty years. Dan's cartoons have appeared in magazines like *Barron's, Good Housekeeping* and, *Reader's Digest*. Dan operates DansCartoons.com on a fulltime basis where he features a new cartoon every day. You can access over 3,000-plus of his cartoons for any professional project. E-mail him at dan@danscartoons.com.

Ruth Rotkowitz is a freelance writer and English teacher. She has published poetry and nonfiction in *Piano Press, Shemom, Expecting, Hopscotch,* and the *Woman's Newspaper of Princeton,* where she served as a staff writer and member of the editorial board. She is currently at work on a novel.

Lahre Shiflet has had her artwork featured in four Chicken Soup for the Soul titles. A high school student, Lahre is an accomplished musician, combining her piano and vocal talents in creating original musical scores on her Mac computer. She is also an aspiring model and actor.

Maggie Lamond Simone is an award-winning writer and graduate of William Smith College and the S. I. Newhouse School of Communications. Her essays have appeared in *Misadventures of Moms and Disasters of Dads; Hello, Goodbye;* and *Cosmopolitan.* She is the author of two children's books and an upcoming memoir.

Laura Smith is the author of the children's book *Cantaloupe Trees* and numerous short stories. She graduated from Miami University with a bachelor's degree in marketing. Laura lives in Oxford, Ohio, with her husband and their four children. Please e-mail her at reds@mindspring.com.

Elva Stoelers is an award-winning Canadian writer. Her work has appeared in *Chicken Soup for the Shopper's Soul*, *Chicken Soup for the Recovering Soul*, and *Recovering Soul Daily Inspirations*. As well as being broadcast on CBC Radio, Elva has been published internationally in many small press parenting magazines.

Lois Greene Stone, writer and poet, has been syndicated worldwide. Poetry and personal essays have been included in hardcover and soft-cover book anthologies. Collections of her personal items/photos/memorabilia are in major museums, including twelve different divisions of the Smithsonian.

Michael Floyd Thompson loves spending time with wife Stephanie and daughter Micah, now four. Whether hiking around their land on "adventures" or snuggling together for family night movies, Micah loves spending time with Daddy. Reach him at P.O. Box 1502, Edmond, OK 73083 or at michael@stateofchange.net.

Stephanie Welcher Thompson is a first-time mom at forty-one, who enjoys life with husband Michael and daughter Micah, now four. A contributor to *Guideposts, Angels on Earth, Positive Thinking*, and *Sweet 16*, her stories have appeared in eight Chicken Soup books. Reach her at P.O. Box 1502, Edmond, OK 73083 or at stephanie@ stateofchange.net.

Jacinda Townsend, a 2003–4 fiction fellow at the University of Wisconsin and a 2002 Hurston Wright Award finalist, has published fiction in numerous literary magazines and anthologies. A former Fulbright fellow and graduate of both Harvard University and the Iowa Writers' Workshop, she teaches at Southern Illinois University.

Cristy Trandahl is a freelance writer and mother of six. She has been a teacher and writer for the nation's leading student progress monitoring company. Today she educates her children at their home in rural Minnesota. Contact her to speak at your mom's group at davecristy@frontiernet.net.

Mary Vallo is a writer, mother of three children, and editor of the regional magazine *The Parent Paper*. She is pursuing a master of arts in writing at Manhattanville College. She lives in Pearl River, New York. Please e-mail her at maryvallo@ optonline.net.

Barbara Warner lives with her husband, Brian, and three children outside Dallas, Texas. A former high school English teacher, she is currently an at-home mother and freelance writer. She also has a sister, Laura, who she didn't mention in this story, but who she loves very much. E-mail her at brian.warner2@gte.net.

Stefanie Wass lives in Hudson, Ohio, with her husband and two girls. She enjoys writing, reading, teaching Sunday school, and spending time with family. Her essays can be found online at www.Heartwarmers.com.

Emily Weaver is a children's book author living in Springfield, Missouri. As a stay-at-home mother of two, her days are filled with imagination and creativity. Emily enjoys traveling, gardening, and cooking. She can be reached by e-mail at emily-weaver@sbcglobal.net.

June Williams is in the process of being broken down by her four grandkids, after being broken in by her two kids! She and her husband, Mac, love to have the whole family visit their little house in Brush Prairie, Washington.

Gloria Wooldridge resides in Prince Edward Island, Canada, with her husband and two daughters. She works part-time as an education assistant and is involved in facilitating small group ministry in her local church. She would like to continue to develop as a writer. Gloria may be contacted at bwhereyouare@gmail.com.

Bob Zahn has had thousands of his cartoons and several of his humor books published. A catalog of his cartoons can be seen at www.cartoonfile.com.

Jeanne Zornes, of Washington State, first encountered motherhood at age thirty-five; her son and daughter are now young adults. She's the author of several books, including one she says her children inspired: *When I Prayed for Patience, God Let Me Have It!* Learn more about her conference speaking at www.allaboutquotes.com.

Permissions *(continued from page iv)*

Beautiful Mess. Reprinted by permission of Heather Michelle Best. ©2006 Heather Michelle Best.

Unplanned Blessings. Reprinted by permission of Catherine Madera. ©2006 Catherine Madera.

I Want My Mom. Reprinted by permission of Linda Sue O'Connell. ©2006 Linda Sue O'Connell.

Completely Us. Reprinted by permission of Kaye Robertson. ©2006 Kaye Robertson.

A Joyous Journey. Reprinted by permission of Rebecca Anne Povich. ©2006 Rebecca Anne Povich.

Twice Blessed. Reprinted by permission of Mary Kathryn Lay. ©1998 Mary Kathryn Lay.

Passing the Baton. Reprinted by permission of Elva Rae Stoelers. ©2005 Elva Rae Stoelers.

The Right Stuff. Reprinted by permission of Dahlynn J. McKowen. ©2006 Dahlynn J. McKowen.

Better than Expected. Reprinted by permission of Cristy Trandahl. ©2006 Cristy Trandahl.

First Night Home. Reprinted by permission of Mary Knight. ©1997 Mary Knight.

What Does Hope Mean to You?. Reprinted by permission of Heather Black. ©2004 Heather Black.

Because He Loved Me. Reprinted by permission of Ginger LeBlanc. ©2006 Ginger LeBlanc.

There's No Place Like Home. Reprinted by permission of Ruth Frances Rotkowitz. ©1984 Ruth Frances Rotkowitz.

Second Fiddle. Reprinted by permission of Mary C. Vallo. ©2006 Mary C. Vallo.

It's Not a Piece of Cake. Reprinted by permission of SG Birch. ©2001 SG Birch.

Needing More than Groceries. Reprinted by permission of Mimi Greenwood Knight. ©1992 Mimi Greenwood Knight.

The Good Doctor. Reprinted by permission of Margaret S. Frezon. ©2006 Margaret S. Frezon.

The Second Greatest Gift. Reprinted by permission of Kathy Partak. ©2006 Kathy Partak.

What Every New Mom Really Needs. Reprinted by permission of Susanna Hickman Bartee. ©2004 Susanna Hickman Bartee.

The Perfect Recording. Reprinted by permission of Jacinda Townsend. ©2006 Jacinda Townsend.

The Bliss of Motherhood. Reprinted by permission of Laura Elizabeth-Abelson Mueller. ©2006 Laura Elizabeth-Abelson Mueller.

A Friend in Need Is Family Indeed. Reprinted by permission of Susan A. Karas. ©2006 Susan A. Karas.